Co. I

314th INFANTRY REGIMENT

79th INFANTRY DIVISION

The combat infantry badge. Airplane pilots get their "wings", paratroopers, get their "paratroop or airborne badge," and the infantry got the combat infantry badge, after they had seen action in combat. The combat infantry badge was handed out by the thousands, and maybe even more than a million received them in WWII, but it is the badge that I am most proud to have earned and worn.

–RJ McDonnell

DOGFACE (slang):

A U.S. Army foot soldier (infantry), especially during WWII

CONTENTS

Age 18 (1943)

PREFACE

O ver the years, as I have related stories of my experiences as a soldier in WWII, listeners often commented, "You should write a book." Namely, my three children, Mary, Bobby, and Laurie urged me to write my stories down. They pushed to the point of buying a tape recorder in the late 1980s so that I could simply talk instead of write. The initial coaxing came from them. Thanks for pushing.

Another strong push came from a Frenchman named Michel (Mike) Cousin. Mike was born and raised in France and now lives in Paris* with his family, including twin granddaughters. Mike was twelve years old when France was liberated, and his memories are strong of German occupational forces, and also of life after the liberation. He served as an officer in the French Army, as did his father. Currently he works as an engineer for General Motors Corporation of France.

My wife and I met Mike through our son. As a college student, Bobby had an internship (1987) at General Motors France, where Mike was his supervisor. While working together the two of

---

*Mike Cousin died August 15, 2008 at the age of 77.

13

them became friends. In the summer of 1987, Mike came to Saginaw, Michigan on business. At the time, General Motors had a number of thriving plant divisions here in Saginaw. Mike was sent to Saginaw with regards to work. Through Bobby, we became aware that Mike would come this way, and we enthusiastically invited him over to our house for dinner. That evening, a friendship ignited, blossoming further when his wife accompanied him on a successive trip.

In 1994, on the 50th anniversary of the invasion, my wife Marguerite and I made a trip to France. The purpose of the trip was to visit friends in addition to catching some of the D-Day commemorative festivities. During this trip we had the pleasure of motoring with Mike Cousin and his wife Monique from Paris to Strasbourg. I am not one to make small talk or converse at length for purposes of filling time, so it is hard for even me to believe that Mike and I talked war stories nonstop on our road trip. At the time Mike mentioned repeatedly that he wished that his father had written down his war stories. The message came through loud and clear—another strong push. Thanks Mike, for your suggestions and nudging.

Work on this document began in longhand. As some of you might know, I tend to write with a pencil, in uppercase letters on yellow legal pads or on backsides of junk mail. Aware of my lo-tech working method, my son Bobby was in town visiting and on this particular occasion, I think it was somewhere around 2000, he walked into the house and plopped down in front of me a brand new device, a computer. He "thought it might help" save time with my writing efforts. He taught me the basics, and continues to guide me to this day. Recently he updated that

OVERVIEW

Bear in mind that this is the story of just one Dogface, mudslinging, clodhopping, M1 rifle-toting, hole-digging, starving, sleep-deprived, over–hiked, ass–dragging, combat infantry, GI doughboy grunt. You might say that I was "E PLURIBUS UNUM" (one from many), and on the flip side of the coin, it was the odd man by far that didn't develop an "IN GOD WE TRUST" while into the thick of things in combat. There were thousands and thousands of us and this is my story as I remember it and not surprisingly, much has remained in my memory.

William Tecumseh Sherman, Civil War general in the Union Army, is credited for the verbalization of the often repeated phrase "War is hell." Audie Murphy, the most decorated soldier of WWII, was in the combat infantry, and titled his book and subsequent movie "To Hell and Back."

Now I would like to put in my two cents worth and add that if you have spent any time at all in WWII wartime combat, as an infantryman, you have lived in hell, and the longer you were there, the more hell you endured. Day after day, week after week and month after month you were not only in hell, but the longer you survived in combat, the deeper you descended into hell.

Subtracting time spent back at the hospital when I was wounded and time near the end of the war when we just sat still and acted like policemen (which is covered toward the end of this document), I managed to live through about eight months of combat duty. So I can say with confidence that I have been there and know what it was like.

As these pages unfold, I hope I am able to convey to you what some of it was like, and by sharing some of my experiences, you, the reader, will better understand what the dogfaces and those around them lived like, endured, and in most cases, survived.

My intent is to tell all of the facts that I remember and to do it in a sometimes humorous way so as not to bore the reader. Please don't get the idea from my style of writing that combat was taken lightly, it wasn't. Combat was as serious as death. I also will avoid painting detailed gory word pictures just for the sake of violent impressions.

Further, please excuse the swear words, as I incorporate them only in the interest of a truer picture of life and atmosphere in the Army and the infantry.

Regarding swear words; Let me tell you what one renowned person had to say regarding servicemen swearing, Ernie Pyle in particular.

During WWII, Ernie Pyle was one of the most liked and admired civilian war journalists in Europe. He lived with and wrote about different Army units, and also some Navy units, stationed in Europe, and it is my belief that he spent more time with the infantry than any other single unit, following them wherever the unit might go.

Ernie Pyle also coauthored a book, "Brave Men," in which he said "The infantry lived like animals and swore more than any other single unit in the Army." I admired his phrase for its accuracy as well as its brevity. The plain simple truth is that we did live like animals, and I can give some insight as to why we swore the way we did.

In basic training, the training cadre created an atmosphere that the King's English wasn't devoid of swear words and as a matter of fact the more and the louder, the better. The tempo of swearing was then enhanced because of the youthful age. Most of the trainees brought the habit right into combat with them. The feelings of camaraderie and "belonging" appeared to grow the more you crowded four letter words into the same sentence, thus swearing became the norm. In reality, there were few things to vent one's feelings over. Some of the tension in combat was relieved by talking, smoking, and swearing; so swearing did have its positive effect.

Postscript on Ernie: When the war in Europe ended, Ernie Pyle transferred to the Pacific theatre of operations where there was still action going on. He was killed over there by a sniper. He is the only civilian that I know of who was awarded the Purple Heart, and deservedly so. It was a nice addition to the Pulitzer Prize that he had been awarded earlier in his career.

Heroes in War: My Opinion

As far as the members of the military were concerned, those who gave their all by losing their lives are the biggest heroes. After the military personnel came those civilians who endured living hell to a degree that we find hard to believe, even after watching documentary motion pictures of their treatment. Those were the itinerants of Europe and the Jews who endured the concentration camps. What an example of "Man's inhumanity to man."

These atrocities were committed under and by Hitler and his regime. History reveals that Joseph Stalin was equally bad or worse, having sent millions to their death.

Next were the military prisoners of war, and from what I've heard, read, and watched on television, more so those in the Pacific Theater under the Japanese than the prisoners taken by the Germans in the European Theater of Operations. And in my evaluation, close on the heels of the POWs was the goddamned infantry. By the way, anyone in or having anything to do with the infantry during WWII always called it the *goddamned* infantry. In looking back now, I don't know whether the severe descriptive adjective *goddamned* was adopted out of sympathy or in search of truth. Maybe that was to be their fate, that they were just plain damned, not by God, but by the mechanics of war.

Addressing emotional scars and spirit of veterans, for ten to fifteen years after the war I could not talk about what I had experienced. I would get worked up or upset inside and as I became somewhat troubled, it would show in my voice. So I just didn't talk about having been in the damned infantry.

A few words here on how emotions can work a person up inside and sometimes even take control for years. These emotional scars happened to prisoners of war, dogfaces and those around them, and anyone else who experienced really traumatic (and I mean traumatic) experiences. Later on, I will cover how external events affect the mind and spirit and create emotional scars. Refer to the chapter on COMBAT FATIGUE.

The emotional scars remain in the back of the mind and have no apparent effect on a person until they are brought forward in some way, like a mention of the events that made the scars, a movie, a book, someone talking about the war, or a newsreel. Newsreels in theaters used to be shown between the main features of a movie. Today, newsreels in theaters are a thing of the past.

A good example of a newsreel reawakening emotional scars happened shortly after I returned from service. I can't recall what the newsreel's subject was, but they showed footage of a lot of dead horses lying along the road in France. The string of dead horses had either been killed by artillery or strafed by airplanes, as there were many corpses close together. Though I was sitting in the theater, I could smell the dead horses. At different times during the war, we walked through city blocks of dead horses lying end-to-end, including during the heat of the summer months when the smell was particularly strong. My memory had retained the association between the sight of the horses and the smell. They say time heals all wounds and I guess it took mine ten to fifteen years to subside.

Reference note: The Germans used a lot of horse-drawn units early on after the invasion but seemed to use them less and less from midsummer on as the war progressed.

Another example of emotional scars occurred when I was watching TV on the fiftieth anniversary of the invasion of Normandy. Some of the veterans choked up as they told their war stories, and a tear or two, which I'm sure hadn't received permission, flowed. I understood. Their emotional scars surely must have run deep.

I'd like to add here that there were more than just the infantry that were placed in harm's way during the ground war in Europe. There were the artillery, tank corps, medics, combat engineers, signal corps, and within the divisions there were reconnaissance groups that, in addition to reconnoitering, also engaged the enemy directly to see who was going to be left occupying the contested ground at the end of the engagement, or to put it more simply, who was going to kick (kill) whose butt for the control of that particular piece of landscape. There are many interesting tales the recon guys have to tell and if you know anyone who has "been there," ask them to share a tale or two, or at least tell you how they operated. I know you won't be disappointed. I'm sure I have missed mentioning others who laid their lives on the line in pursuit of their duties and to them I say I'm sorry not to have listed them. Now...onward.

I will cover my pre-induction period as it had some effect on my service time. I will also introduce you to my family and try to give you (the reader) a little taste of the times.

PRE-ARMY PERIOD

War Effort

I graduated from high school in June of 1943 at which time I was eighteen years and one month old. The entire country was wrapped up in an all-out war effort. WWII had been in progress a little over a year and a half, since December 7, 1941. Patriotism on the part of the American people was at its peak. Most people had the will, desire and resolve to help in America's all out effort to win the war. All priorities went to the military, and the common goal was to beat the "dirty" Japs and the same for the "no-good" Germans. Posters were everywhere: "BUY BONDS", "LOOSE LIPS SINK SHIPS", "I'M COUNTING ON YOU", "DON'T DISCUSS", "THE MILITARY NEEDS YOU", "UNCLE SAM WANTS YOU", "THE NAVY WANTS YOU", "BE A MARINE", "JOIN THE NAVY AND SEE THE WORLD", to mention a few.

While still in school, we had junk days on which every student brought every piece of scrap metal to school that he or she could scrounge, by whatever means. I'm sure that some students went overboard in the spirit of the endeavor and snuck things from home that were still on the useful list. The scrap was thrown on top of a single pile to see how big and high the pile would grow.

Gasoline was being rationed. Time permitting, people would walk or take a bus, even if they had cars. Other things on the tightly rationed list were rubber (including all civilian vehicle tires), butter, sugar, meat, and anything made from those basic ingredients. The things that weren't being rationed weren't being manufactured, such as automobiles and car replacement parts. Civilian clothing manufacturing was held to a minimum, as well as shoes, leather goods, silk scarves and hose, etc. The military needed silk for making parachutes, and it took a lot of stockings to make one parachute. If the manufactured goods went for military goods or personnel, fine. If the goods were for civilian use, "sorry, our boys in service need that." The same applied to most food items. If the customer became irate, the standard answer was "there's a war on, ya know."

People were tightening their belts and doing without. People my age and older knew what it was like to live lean, as we had experienced the trials of the Depression, and more so our parents, as they not only went without, but had the responsibility of the well-being of their children. The news media was completely behind the war effort and were cooperative and conscientious about not printing anything that would aid the enemy. The country, the government (both parties), and the press were working together. This may be hard to believe in view of how things are being handled today, but it did go on back then.

With all the shortages going on a new phrase was creeping into our vocabulary: "black market." In spite of all the good that was going on, there were always a few bad apples to be found. If they couldn't buy it on the open market, some paid a higher price and bought it illegally.

The Plant

It wasn't money that was stopping people from having things, as the national unemployment level was hovering around three percent, about the lowest in history. If you didn't work, it was because you were making a deliberate effort not to. For instance, a couple of days after graduation, I applied for a job at the foundry here in big-town Saginaw, Michigan. I filled out an application, was given a physical during which they determined I could stand up, breathe, and walk. I was given an identification badge, told what time to report for work the next morning and was directed as to which door would get me back on the street. When I got home, I told my dad at suppertime that I had taken a job at the foundry, and he said, "Why? The Transmission plant where I work pays five cents an hour more and you can ride to work in the same car pool with me." So, the next morning I went through the same routine at the Transmission plant, and started there the next day. It was definitely a workers' market. Any man who was physically able and of military age had two choices, work or go into the military, and as for me, I was about to learn the meaning of "work" in a plant.

The pay structure was based on working nine hours a day, six days a week, ninety-five cents an hour, with time and a half for overtime. The arithmetic comes out to fifty-seven dollars and ninety cents for the week, before taxes.

The war effort had converted the plant from automobile transmission manufacturing to a forge plant for the production of airplane parts. The primary parts produced were airplane propeller blades, motor blocks, and landing gear parts, and all were aluminum. Forging means the raw cast aluminum was heated to a high temperature (if it were steel it would be red hot, but being aluminum, it didn't change color as it was heated) and then the parts were put, one piece at a time, into a vertical "hammer." The hammer held two dies: one was stationary and the second moved up and down. Each die had the inverse shape of that of the finished part to be. Some propeller blades were nine feet long, and the hammers that hammered them out were huge. The top die, which was the moveable one, weighed somewhere between six and nine tons, and the bottom (stationary) die weighed the same. When they got to smacking those two together, with a nine-foot long solid aluminum bar (about five to six inches in diameter) in between, the casual observer kind of looked around for the nearest exit. And noisy! When a hammer was running, the dishes on the tables and in the cupboards of the homes in a three-block radius rattled, and the pictures on the walls never hung straight. The foundations of homes in the near vicinity started to become questionable as to their integrity. On a damp evening, the noise of the hammer could be heard for a three-mile radius. The only reason the noise wasn't heard during the day at three miles was that the normal ambient noise masked it. I had the dubious honor of working on and around that hammer during my three months prior to service. I was just a grunt, being that I was a new hire, and as such was shifted around a lot. Truth be known, they worked my six foot, one hundred fifty pound butt off. I didn't have much of one to begin with, but that place surely wanted every ounce of it.

One day they had me taking parts out of a furnace using a pair of tongs and carrying them ten feet to a smaller hammer than previously described. The parts were about fifteen pounds a piece, and the tongs used to handle them were approximately five feet long. The parts had to be heated in the furnace, which had an exterior door that was roughly four to five feet square. The interior measured five feet square, with six inch holes on the interior backside. To load the furnace, parts were thrown into a pile inside the front door. After the parts were brought up to temperature at 800 degrees, the hammer was started and our five-person crew went to work. Part of my job involved approaching the furnace to rake a part into position in order to grab it with the tongs. The plant wasn't air-conditioned, and in the summertime, the exterior doors were left open to pull in any breeze from the outdoors. When there happened to be even the slightest trace of breeze, the air was sucked through those holes, intensifying the heat pouring out of the furnace. The heat was so hot, it came close to burning my nose hairs! On any given day, by lunchtime, I was beat. Between the physical challenges and the heat blasting from the furnace, I could barely summon enough energy to climb the stairs to the cafeteria.

Another day, I was assigned a job lifting seventy pound castings. Measuring off my body, the range-of-motion involved was from floor level to a little over belt high—when my pants weren't drooping. I didn't have any hips either. (No butt and no hips. What do you expect for one hundred-fifty pounds?) This job required loading the front end of a furnace that had a conveyor belt. The belt took the parts through the furnace, my job was to place the castings on the belt. Sweating and grunting like mad, I was having a heck of a time keeping up with that conveyor. Sometime past mid-morning, my foreman walked by. I called him over, suggesting the gorilla over there in the tank top and I change places now and then. This gorilla guy, who looked like Hercules, was seemingly underworked, working a trim press. Every now and again, after what seemed like an extraordinary time lapse, gorilla-man hit the black button on the trim press. I'm sure if that guy ate a small banana for lunch he would gain more calories than he had expended. The foreman looked at me blankly and said, "I can't do that." So I asked him if I could have a pass home. He replied, "Would you rather work or go in the Army?" I told him, "In two weeks I go to Detroit for my physical." As he walked away he said over his shoulder, "Good boy, good boy." I mumbled something under my breath. I can't remember exactly what I said as I went back to lifting those damned heavy castings, but I'm sure it was something colorfully appropriate, even if that loud-ass hammer was pounding in the background.

Characteristic of those my age, I was no exception to burning the candle at both ends. One week during the three months at the plant, it happened that there was a party every night. They were thrown in honor of some friend who was leaving for service (Army, Navy, or Marines). Over the course of this particular week, the sack-time hours I clocked when added together equaled roughly one night's sleep. Saturday morning came 'round when the alarm went off. I managed to roll out of bed onto my feet, but I couldn't wake up enough to find my work pants. My mom saw all of it, my fractured state, my scrambling. She was well aware of my partying schedule and the hours I was keeping. And now here she was, witnessing my dilemma. I had no idea how she'd respond. Unblinkingly, she declared, "You go back to bed and go in to work at noon." Surprised, I asked, "And what about dad? What will he say?" She replied, "Don't worry, I'll take care of him." Dad's cardinal rule was well known by us kids; "play and party if you like, but go to work, and be on time."

Recalling my dad's stories, often laden with embellishments, it makes me laugh to think about two of his favorites: "One time I dug a hole so crooked I fell out of it!" and another, "Back on the farm during the lean days, we would eat raw navy beans for breakfast, drink water for lunch, and swell up for supper."

When I left the transmission plant, I had a military leave of absence. After the service, I returned to the plant, this time manufacturing car parts. I was granted another leave about six months after returning to go to radio school under the GI Bill of Rights. Six years later, returning to the Saginaw Steering Gear division of General Motors, I learned that all of my work time plus the leave time was credited, and counted toward retirement time and eligibility pay. All right!

In hindsight, I was glad I did three months of bull work in that sweatshop. The job managed to whip me into shape enough that when in the Army, at least for the first part, I thought I was on vacation.

FAMILY

There were twelve kids in my family, nine boys and three girls, with a twenty-two year age difference between the oldest and the youngest. Four of us were in service during WWII; three more followed during peacetime.

Below is a list of the brothers that served, with "in" dates, discharge or "out" dates, and total months served.

- Allen (Ott) Lawrence: in 9-22-42, out 5-2-46 = 43 months

- Lynden (Lynn) Thomas: in 1-27-43, out 12-8-45 = 34 months

- Edward (Ed) Gerard: in 6-9-43, out 4-8-46 = 34 months

- Robert Joseph: in 9-17-43, out 1-6-46 = 28 months

- Lyle Alexander: in 2-5-46, out 5-12-47 = 16 months

- Patrick Wendell: in 5-5-52, out date unknown = ? months

- Michael Dennis: in 7-12-61, out 12-22-64 = 41 months

Out of the nine boys, the two that didn't serve were brother Hazen, who was not required to serve due to poor eyesight, and Donald James, who died at the age of four in a freak accidental fall. None of my sisters opted for the military life. The Army never wrote to say it needed them and the girls never wrote the Army, as the feeling was mutual. Mary Lou and Irene did choose a regimented life by volunteering for a religious life and becoming Dominican Catholic nuns.

Brother Ott was the first to go "in." Ott had poor eyesight and because of it, he was put on limited service, which meant that he would serve his time in the good ol' U. S. of A. He was taught to shoot a rifle left handed because his left eye was the better of the two. He was placed in the MPs (the military police) and issued a sidearm (probably a .45 automatic). Ott put in most of his time on the West Coast, and being there, was exposed to Army, Navy, and Marine personnel, as well as some of the Canadian military. After he left the service, he would tell us stories of his experiences while serving. He talked about how frequently the military personnel were drunk, on leave, or had passes. Their attitude was "for today," or "tonight we get drunk and raise hell, for tomorrow we don't know what." Some of the personnel were just plain flat out mean, in search of a fight, and there was plenty of down-and-dirty fighting that went on. I remember a couple of Ott stories, one of which had to do with a buddy of his trying to quiet down an inebriated Canadian soldier. The soldier was wearing standard Canadian Government Issue hobnailed boots. The Canuck threw a punch knocking the MP flat and was all prepared, with his right leg back, to deliver a hobnailed boot to the head. The MP rolled away and stopped with his forty-five out and aimed, saying, "You kick and you're dead." They had some of those "Make my day" guys in the MPs, too.

Another story had to do with Ott and some other guy going at it, when the other guy grabbed Ott by the neck and had him bent over backwards on the hood of some vehicle. The guy made his second mistake (his first being picking a fight with an MP): he had his finger in Ott's mouth. I think the way Ott put it was "I damn near bit his finger off, before that guy let go."

There were no Purple Hearts awarded to him and his fellow military police, just bruises of the same color. I think I would be safe in saying that all military personnel were not saints, especially when they were on pass and in town to drink and raise a bit of hell.

Brother Lynn was second to obey the call of duty. He was in his second year of college, at the University of Detroit, on an athletic scholarship. They made him captain of the junior varsity basketball team from the get-go, so you might say he had a few moves of his own. He was good, and the draft board wanted him too. Guess who won out?

Lynn became a designated guest of the glorified (A.K.A. goddamned) infantry and was assigned to the 35th Infantry Division, a heavy weapons platoon. He became a member of a five man (don't quote me) team that worked an 81 mm mortar. One man carried the tube and its associated two legs, another man carried the heavy base plate, and the remaining three men were ammunition bearers. Lynn was wounded once, for which he received a Purple Heart. He was also awarded the Bronze Star medal for meritorious action above and beyond the call of duty. I'm sorry to say, I don't remember the details: sorry Lynn. The heavy weapons units traveled and stayed behind the rifle platoons, as the range of their weapons was (I'm guessing) a

---

*Here they are, in birth order, Edward Gerard (b. 1919), Allen (Ott) Lawrence (b. 1921), Lynden (Lynn) Thomas (b. 1922), me, Robert Joseph (b. 1925), Lyle Alexander (b. 1927), Hazen Stewart (b. 1930), Patrick Wendell (b. 1931), Marilyn Jean (b. 1932), Mary Lou (b. 1934), Donald James (b. 1936), Irene Bernadette (b. 1940), Michael Dennis (b. 1942).

mile or less. Years after we were out, Lynn paid me a compliment by saying, "You know, you guys really went through hell." He then continued commenting by comparing the conditions my bunch lived under compared to his. A little more about Lynn and me crossing paths in combat comes later.

Next it was Ed's turn at bat. Ed had finished his college schooling at General Motors Institute of Technology and was a foreman at Saginaw Steering Gear. Since S.S.G. was making critical parts for the war effort, Ed was given a couple of deferments. His patriotic attitude brought on his decision to give up the money and security of home front plant life to don the togs of "You're in the Army Now." To the best of my knowledge, he and Mike were the only of my brothers who volunteered. I am uncertain in Pat's case—I don't know if he went in as a volunteer or was called.

In spite of Ed's college training and high scores on his Army induction test, he was put in the Army Corps of Engineers. This engineering unit did not sit at drafting boards conceiving and drawing plans; rather, they executed others' plans. They were given—no, the word isn't "given"—they were issued shovels, picks, hoes, and rakes; the tools to build sidewalks, blacktop roads, military emplacements, etc. After his training in the U.S., Ed spent ninety percent or more of his overseas time in England either constructing or demolishing something. Once, when he and his fellow Army corps members were working on repairing a road, the actor James Cagney passed slowly in a car. He was being driven through the work area where they were busy blacktopping. He stopped to talk to "the boys." James Cagney had his own way of saying "you boys." Noticing their skin slick with oil, sweat running down their muscular frames, he said something to the effect of how good work was for the body. Though the crew kept comments to themselves, I'm sure they were thinking, "you may be right, but I'll trade places with you or even your driver, anytime!"

After all was said and done, Ed and his outfit were lucky to have remained in England. Ed's and my paths crossed twice while we were overseas, and I'll address that later, also.

Fourth to bat, but surely not in the cleanup position, was yours truly. Putting on Army khaki, the word was "Say goodbye to civilian life, for you, too, 'are in the Army now.'"

As the above dates show, Lyle (Ace) went in after WWII and was the first to serve in peacetime. Lyle chose the Army and served in the engineering branch also, played basketball for the Army, and spent some of his time working in aerial photography, layout, and interpretation. When asked about any other specifics as to his time in service, he always says, "I could tell you a lot more, but then I would have to shoot you." I don't know what was so secretive about playing basketball on an Army team, but then again you know the Army's way of doing things. I'm sure the Army took advantage of Lyle and some of his sharp moves, and vice versa. Go get 'em, Ace.

For brother Pat, the Army placement committee decided to get a little variety going, so he was put in the Signal Corps. You might compare them and their work to electric power linemen, as they were taught how to climb (wooden) poles and string wires from the tops of them. If it had been wartime, this type of work would be done behind the lines. As the Signal Corps got near the infantry (and they did get on top of us when the situation called for it) the communication lines (wires) were strung on the ground. In combat they did a good job of running that wire from spools as they ran, walked, or crawled. Many times they were walking backwards. Sometimes, when we went back for rations and it was pitch dark, we would pick up a communication line and let it slide through our hand as we worked our way along. Going back it was the same. Other times, while walking in the dark, a communication line reestablished our sense of direction, so those lines were used for more than voice communications.

When enemy artillery fire knocked out a communication line and one of the linemen had to find and repair it, he did the same thing we did, he would walk along and let the line slide through his hand until he came to the break. Those guys, at times, literally and figuratively laid their butts on the line. They endured sniper fire, rifle and artillery fire, right along with the rest of us.

And now brother Mike, the last but surely not the least, was purely a volunteer. Mike enlisted in the United States Air Force. By this time the Air Force had been split off from the Army, and was an entity in itself. Mike did his basic training in Texas, moved to Mississippi, and then on to Germany for three years, working all the time in ground radar.

Let me add a word here about the family and signing letters. I don't know who started it, but while in service, at the end of those letters we sent home, we used numbers instead of names. Since I was fourth-born, I was simply No. 4. I don't think Ed started it, as I can't think of him referring to himself (rightfully) as No 1. Face to face we might say, "I'm number one," but not in a letter. When Mike's turn came, he joined in by signing off as No. 12, and then he would add "the last of the dirty dozen." The numbering system has been good, and it has lasted, including the girls, even yet today.

Let me add here that our dad and mom never went to the train depot to see any of us off. To quote my mom, "I'll say goodbye to you here in the kitchen, and I'll be here in the kitchen when you return." Sure enough, when I did return (they knew I was coming but not exactly when), my mom was standing at the stove, with her back to me, as I opened the door. My eyes went past her on the first sweep and then came back to her. Her hair had turned completely gray. She, too, had had her moments and days of mental stress worrying about her sons in the military. Her sister-in-law, in Canada, had lost three sons. All three had been pilots in the British Air Force. That only added to my mother's fears as to what "might happen" to her boys, along with, of course, reading the constant updating of the killed and wounded in the newspaper. She couldn't control the color of her hair, but otherwise she bore her cross of duty well. Any emotions that my father might have had, he tried (successfully) never to show, as was his way. Verbalizing, no matter what the occasion, was not his way. A smile would just have to do.

YOU'RE IN THE ARMY NOW

Physicals

About two weeks prior to leaving for service, all draftees were bused to Detroit for a complete physical. This would be our first time to stand in line(s) buck naked. Embarrassing, you bet! Most of us were eighteen or nineteen, and some of us had been exposed to communal showers having played sports, but parading naked, no. As with most other things, we would learn to adapt. While in service, especially if we were leaving or arriving at a new camp, we had to have another physical. The Army wasn't interested in checking the vital signs: its priority and attention went toward checking for venereal diseases. I remember the "physical" at the embarkation camp. For some reason, it and the one on the boat coming home are clearer. At the embarkation camp, the order was to fall out with shoes, overcoat, and a spoon, nothing else. I think it was the first time for that particular uniform. (Here comes a whole damn company of flashers.)

Reference note: The Army used letters to designate different types of uniforms. For instance, class A was your formal and best uniform, used for retreat formations, parades, and whenever anyone left camp.

After forming up in columns outside, we were marched a few blocks to a big building. Lining up in front of the doctor, who was usually seated on a chair, we had only to open our overcoats to perform the necessary moves. Yes, there was a lot of flashing going on that day, and I'll bet you want to know what that spoon was for. There is venereal disease of the mouth. The next line led to a doctor, to whom you handed your spoon. He used it for a tongue depressor, to examine the mouth and throat.

The other time that stands out is when we were on the boat coming home. I know we were in our bare feet and the guy in front of me had a venereal disease and the attendants kept cautioning me, "Don't step there and don't sit here, etc."

After the physical in Detroit, we were sworn into the Army and I remember there was one guy in the group that did not stand nor raise his right hand during the swearing in ceremony. The officer in charge noticed toward the end and told the guy, "You didn't do what you were supposed to, but you're sworn in anyhow."

Camp Custer

The next step was to board a train in Saginaw, along with all the other draftees for a free ride to Camp Custer. Camp Custer, located just outside of Battle Creek, Michigan, was, I believe, my first ride on a train where I knew what was going on. The only train trip previous to this was when I was approximately two months old and my mother, along with my three older brothers, were migrating from their farm outside of a small village called Apple Hill, Ontario, Canada. That train trip was about five hundred miles long. We were on our way to join my Dad in Detroit, Michigan. Dad was working at Cadillac Motors. He too thought he was on vacation working just forty hours a week as opposed to endless hours on the farm in Canada.

At Camp Custer we were issued our clothes and boots along with a duffel bag to store and carry them. I remember that everywhere we went as a group, some loudmouth standing off a ways would be yelling, "You'll be sorry." Hell, I was still on vacation since leaving the "prop" shop. I'll say once again, I was glad I had done time there.

One other thing about the camp, everyone complained (in Army talk you didn't "complain," you "bitched") about the food. Not me! I ate it all, with the exception of eggplant, which I kind of gagged down, never having eaten that soft mushy stuff at home. One thing I did find funny in the mess hall was that the cups were a little larger than average, and they were thick white or milk glass and had no handles. Very practical, really.

I don't remember how long the stay was at General George Armstrong Custer's camp. We were all given an IQ test. The Army called it the AGCT, or the Army General Classification Test. We were also checked to see if we knew Morse code. I must have done decently on the AGCT, as I was asked if I wanted to go into the Army Air Corps. I answered with a quick "Sure." After passing the color blindness test, I was asked, "Were you born in the U. S. of A.?" I answered, "No, Canada." He said, "That's all, you can go back to the line you came from." Now wasn't that short and sweet?

I mustn't forget, at Camp Custer they taught us how to make a bed, Army-style. When you make a bed Army-style it has to have square corners. The sheets and the top blanket have to be turned down a specified distance from the head, with the seam tucked under. And most importantly the sheets and top blanket have to be tucked under until the blanket was tight enough to make a two bit coin (a quarter) bounce. And by the way, we were never allowed to sit or lie on the bed until the work day was over.

The same invitation to join the Air Corps came later when I was in basic training. This time I said "Sure" faster and gave it a little more enthusiasm. I had another mental test, a physical, and a hearing before a board of officers. I was told to go back to my barrack and watch the bulletin board for transfer information, probably within two weeks. Hot shit, I'm moving out—BZZT, WRONG. Within two weeks, the GENERAL NOTICE on the bulletin board read, "No troops will be transferred from ground corps to air corps until further notice." Not long after that, I was approached again and asked if I would be interested in going into the ASTP, or the Army Specialized Training Program. I don't recall falling to my knees and grasping the inquirer by the knees while looking up with pleading, tear-filled eyes and beseechingly moaning "yes, yes, yes," but I did answer in the affirmative. ASTP was something like college courses to fit you into some special Army categories. In any case I never heard from them again. Pity! Let's get back to Camp Custer.

Reference note: General G. A. Custer, in 1876, attacked the Sioux Indians, who were camped on the Little Big Horn River in Montana. At the end of the battle, Custer, along with 247 of the men under him, were dead. The only living thing at the end of the battle, on the Army's side, was one officer's horse. General Custer had made another mistake, one of many, and his last. I wonder why they named a camp after him.

From Camp Custer, it was a longer train ride, taking me to new records, distance-wise, in a southwesterly direction. We were on the train two or more days. The scenery as we traveled west was new, and at times, awesome. Rumors as to our destination were flying around faster than food in a cafeteria food fight. When we did arrive at our destination, it was past suppertime and into the dark of the evening. We were disheveled, dirty, and tired from being cooped up in the train for days, and in no mood for company when the command reverberated through the car, "EVERYBODY OUT!" Bear in mind, the guiding word to all recruits from pre-induction through Camp Custer was, "Stay out of, avoid, steer clear of the infantry."

BASIC TRAINING

Arrival

I don't believe the train we were on was at a station of any kind when it stopped, so there were no signs to tell us where we were, but in short order we learned that we were at Camp Wolters, Texas (sometimes called Camp Walters). It is in the north central part of the state, about forty miles due west of Fort Worth, and just outside a small town called Mineral Wells. We were met by a bunch of yelling, swearing cadres that double timed us for maybe a quarter of a mile, from the train stop to our barracks, duffel bags on our shoulders. We knew it was late, and that the yellers probably had had a long day, but there was no reason to take it out on us. Like I said, we weren't in the mood for company, either. After a lot more yelling, we were issued all bedding material and assigned barracks and beds.

We were then howled at to "fall in outside," meaning "gather on the parade ground." The parade ground was a little larger than half a city block and lined on all four sides with barracks. The ground was barren and there were no footprints in the concrete-like clay. Any life that had been in that ground had long since been extinguished by the herds of soldiers tromping it down in their oversized Army boots. We would get to know every inch of that super-packed earth. It was where we would learn how to do close order drill: back and forth, up and down, and around 'n' around, hour after hour. As instructed, we would be doing this until every man gets it right and then more after that. After falling out of our newly assigned barracks, and moving on to the parade ground, we were told to sit. An officer stepped up on a lighted platform and with microphone in hand, started: "MEN, YOU ARE IN THE GODDAMNED INFANTRY. YOU HEARD ME RIGHT, I SAID THE GODDAMNED INFANTRY!" See, I told you they always used that word before "infantry," and this officer was on a public address system. My thought: "10-4 ... and, oh shit!"

He then outlined for us what the next thirteen weeks of basic training would be. Part of the info he doled out was (using his words) "We will hike your asses off!" and (quoting again) "There will be times when you will want to quit and drop off to the side of the road. Don't. Just keep following that asshole in front of you. Each of you has a safety valve that kicks in when you have had too much. Keep going until it blows."

Reference note: Most of the time, the training officers accompanied us on our hikes, even on our longest (25 mile) hike.

The basic training we were to receive was to make us fit to be replacements for infantry personnel killed or wounded in combat. The training was slanted toward going to the Pacific Theater of Operations against the Japs. We were never told that, but surmised it after having instructions on malaria, which is spread by the female Anopheles mosquito. Another clue was the extensive training in using the bayonet, which we all loved so much. Getting serious for a moment, word was that the Japanese were very skilled in the use of the bayonet and used it often, as there was a lot of close in fighting going on in the Pacific Theater of Operations.

Reference note: The Jap bayonet was one quarter to one half again the length of ours, which gave them a little advantage. This would have given them an advantage over us, had their reach been the same as the Westerners.

The purpose of basic training was to condition us physically, program us mentally to follow orders, teach us how to fire different weapons, how to dismantle and clean weapons, defense against a bayonet, how to kill with a bayonet, more how to kill with a bayonet, more yet on how to kill with a bayonet, hand to hand combat, military field problems, use of the compass, and to understand the Articles of War. The Articles of War give definition to crimes for military personnel and describes the punishment due for said crimes. It was mandatory to have them read to us every 30 or 60 days. The training was thorough and physically taxing to say the least. One of the things that got to me was holding the M1 rifle up in front, chest high and double-timing with it there. After about two to three blocks the shoulders would start to burn and the arms would get numb.

M1 Rifle

The M1 rifle weighed nine and one half pounds, empty without the bayonet. The bayonet weighed one pound. When we were issued our rifles, we were told to memorize the serial number on it so that we would always know our own rifle. It then became our constant companion during "basic," and even more so in combat. During basic training we didn't eat, sleep, or go to the bathroom with our rifles, but in combat we did. The classes we had on dismantling and reassembling the M1 were called "studying the nomenclature of the M1," and yes, we did get to the point that we could do it in the dark, even blindfolded. The classes were held in an open field on a blanket spread on the ground.

The M1 was a semi-automatic rifle, meaning it reloaded itself after firing the first round (bullet), but you had to pull the trigger each time to make it fire. The magazine or clip that was loaded in the M1 contained eight rounds and as you fired the last round of the clip, the empty metal clip proper would eject, leaving the clip chamber open, and the bolt would be back ready for another loaded clip to be inserted. When a new clip was inserted the bolt moved forward automatically leaving a new round in the chamber to be fired. The M1 was a sturdy rifle and could take a lot of abuse. They said that after being immersed in water it fired even better for a while. It did have to be dried out and cleaned after having been dunked. Under combat conditions of walking all day in the rain, which we did at times, we just carried our rifles, slung over the shoulder, upside down. In qualifying with the M1, we fired it from one hundred through five hundred yard distances. The specs for the M1 say it has an effective range of 440 yards. We fired them, accurately, at 500 yards and were told the maximum killing range was 700 yards. To "fire for record" means you fired five rounds at each distance. The score was then tallied and entered into your permanent Army record. You would do the same with each different weapon, whether it was a twenty-two caliber rifle, a carbine, or a forty-five caliber handgun.

From http://www.rt66.com/~korteng/SmallArms/m1rifle.html
(© Kortegaard Engineering):

US Rifle Caliber .30 M1 Garand

Operation: Semiautomatic, Gas Operated

Caliber: .30 (.30-06)

Length: 43.6 in. (1103 mm)

Weight unloaded: 9 lb 8 oz (4.37 kg)

Barrel: 24 in. 4 grooves, right hand twist

Magazine: 8 round internal box, clip loaded, clip ejected after last round fired

Muzzle: velocity 2800 fps, 2650 ft-lb Muzzle Energy

500 yds: 1918 fps, 1362 ft-lbs

Ammunition: .30-06 Cartridge, Ball, caliber 30, M2, 150 gr, 50 gr charge

Effective Range: 440 yds

Classification: "Standard" from 1936 until M14 adopted in 1957

Total production: Approx. 4,040,000

"In my opinion, the M1 Rifle is the greatest battle implement ever devised."

LGEN George S. Patton, Jr.

The M1 Garand is a full blown combat rifle with maxiumum range of 3,200 meters and maximum effective range of 400 meters.....or the greatest distance at which the weapon can be expected to fire accurately to inflict casualties or damage. Fully loaded with 8-round en bloc clip, cleaning kit in butt stock, sling and with stock of dense GI issue wood the M1 weighed in at 11-1/4 lbs. The M1 came into production in 1936 using the .30-06 rifle cartridge.

The M1 was the designated service rifle of World War II and the Korean War for the United States Military. It was designed for semi-automatic fire using a spring steel clip containing 8 rounds. This is where the term "clip" originated. All other rifles used a detachable or fixed magazine. (There is some discussion on whether this is accurate, if you have a comment, please enter it on our Bulletin Board.) The M1 Garand was designed for long range accuracy i.e. battle zero was set for any target less than 200 yards It was the only rifle that had fully adjustable i.e. windage and elevation, rear sights.

The M1C, manufactured by Springfield Armory in late 1944-1945, mounted either a M81 or M82 scope, a T4 leather cheek pad, and an M2 flash hider.

The The original rear sight of the M1 would not hold adjustments very well, so a locking bar was added in late 1942 which could be tightened after sights were set.

The US Rifle M1 was the first semiautomatic rifle to be the standard small arm of the US Military, requiring a trigger pull to fire a round but automatically chambering the next round. This not only greatly increased the rate of fire over bolt-action rifles, but made it far easier to reacquire a target after each round. It was also the first semiautomatic rifle to be adopted by a major military power. It was the product of a genuine genius, John Cantius Garand. While the M1 Rifle was never officially referred to as the Garand, it is known by no other name so widely. First adopted in 1936, the M1 Rifle served the US in World War II, Korea, a host of "police actions" and interventions, and, in the hands of allies, in the Vietnam War. Even there the US Army fielded accurized sniper M1 rifles even though the M1 had by that time been supplanted by the M14 and later the M16.

To many the M1 Rifle has a classic elegance and grace characteristic of a bygone era, when steel was forged in white heat and walnut was carefully shaped for both form and function. "There will never be again such a rifle, so brimming with the genius of an individual mind, so well constructed to outlive us all, so sculpted as to ask the hand to caress."

Criticisms of the M1 are its weight, limited ammunition supply, and that single rounds could not be pushed in (8 round clip, or nothing) , although this is actually possible. Also, the spent clip was automatically ejected after the last round was fired, making a distinctive sound, which could be fatal in close quarter or sniper operations. Partially loaded or fully loaded clips could be ejected by pulling the operating rod handle all the way back and then pushing the clip latch on the left side of the receiver. In the heat of close action it was possible to do this accidentally, as by pressing the latch with the left hand while firing from the hip.

As a supplement to the Garand the M1 Carbine was developed. It was totally different design philosophy with a smaller, less powerful cartridge and an effective range of 300 yds max. It weighed almost exactly 1/2 that of the M1 Garand. In many ways you could think of the M1 Carbine as a moderately powerful, two-handed, long-barreled auto pistol with a shoulder stock.

(*Verbatim from FM 23-5 U.S. Rifle Caliber .30, M1*)

Disassembly into the Three Main Groups:

A. The three main groups are the trigger housing group, the barrel and receiver group and the stock group.

B. To disassemble the rifle into the three main groups, first insure that the weapon is clear and then allow the bolt to go forward by depressing the follower with the right thumb and allowing the bolt to ride forward over the follower assembly. (note: careful, M1s are always hungry and eat thumbs).

C. Place the rifle butt against the left thigh, sights to the left. With the thumb and forefinger of the right hand, pull downward and outward on the rear of the trigger guard. Swing the trigger guard out as far as it will go and lift out the trigger housing group.

D. To separate the barrel and receiver from the stock lay the weapon on a flat surface with the sights up, muzzle to the left. With the left hand, grasp the rear of the receiver and raise the rifle. With the right hand, give a downward blow, grasping the small of the

stock. **This will separate the stock group from the barrel and receiver group.**

The M1 is a robust weapon.

Physical Training

Now I'll address the physical part of basic training. Our longest
hike was 25 miles. It was done during our 9th or 10th week. We
knew it was scheduled but did not know when it would take
place. One night around seven or eight in the evening, and after
a normal day's routine, we were told to fall out (to the parade
ground) with full field pack, M1 rifle, bayonet, canteen full of
water, etc. No one ever told you to fill your canteen: you either
kept it full or did without. Water was never a real problem for us
during basic training because it was late fall and early winter,
which made water easy to find.

After standing in formation on the parade ground, we were
told we were going on a long hike and that it would be a tactical march, no talking (even during breaks) and no smoking.
Smoking was normally permitted only during breaks and during non-work hours.

> *Reference note: During the normal workday, the Army al-
> ways took a ten minute break out of each hour. It didn't
> make any difference what we did; it was always 50 minutes
> on then 10 minutes off.*

As it got dark and as we were walking unpaved roads through
open and wooded areas, a connecting file was established. A
connecting file means two to four men would be spaced between
the last man of one platoon and the front man of the following
platoon. Why? When it's dark out, one platoon might turn a
corner and the following platoon might keep going straight.
Also, if a verbal command is to be passed back (whispered, as

it is during a tactical march) the connecting file is used to get the word from platoon to platoon. This march was in a column of two's, with one column on each side of the road.

Reference note: We were actually trained on passing a message from the front of a column to the back and vice-versa. The idea was to do it as accurately as possible. When practiced, it's revealing and funny what happens to even a simple message when it is passed person to person down a line, and whispered messages were really subject to whole-sale corruption.

As luck would have it, I was chosen to be the first man in the connecting file, behind the platoon ahead. About the third hour out, the lieutenant, who was the last man walking in the platoon in front of us, started falling asleep and walking off the road. (We walked for eight or nine hours that night.) I'd catch up and shake him. The first time he did it he whispered, "Good, keep me awake, I was out last night." Wow, a lieutenant got informal with me!

I'm sure I slept during the last five or so miles myself. When we had about two hours to go, I started to fall asleep. Hiking so long in the dark, with the moon shining through the trees, made the trees look like an endless building, with dimly lit windows. This sets up and enhances the pre-sleep period, as the repetitive vertical lines become hypnotic. Anyone who says you can't walk in your sleep should try an all-night hike, and if that doesn't do it, add sixty to seventy pounds of equipment on your back.

When we returned to camp, the first order of business was to take off our shoes and socks, lie on our back with our feet over the end of our cots. The lieutenant had to examine every hiker's feet. In the infantry it was stressed, "You have to take care of your feet, this part of the Army travels on them."

We then sacked out until around 7:30 AM and must have had three or four glorious hours of sleep when someone bellowed, "FALL OUT, FALL OUT, IN STANDARD WORKDAY UNIFORM!" Being stiff and groggy we didn't make it out as fast as the yellers wanted. After being bitched out, we were then marched a mile to listen to some speech in a theater. It wasn't even a Mickey Mouse film. (Mickey Mouse was an Army expression for a film on venereal disease. We saw many.) When we got back to our barracks, we had to practice falling in and out of our barracks because we had done it so slowly at 7:30. There is nothing like coddling the troops. It is during a time like this that we really bitched about anything and everything. It was good to have friends, comrades, or buddies that you could bitch with. We would let all hang out, all the pent up emotions and feelings. It was much better than keeping it inside. The Army always said, "A bitching soldier is a happy soldier." When a bitching session really got going, someone always came up with another way of complaining and it would bring about a laugh, which in turn would help change the mood.

As luck would have it, a "short endurance hike" was to be included in our schedule that day. After a two to three mile hike out, we were on break when told that we would now do a speed hike. This was done on a blacktop road which was quite hilly. Outfitted in full field packs, we did three miles in 33 minutes. The hard part was on the legs. They stiffen like boards and it's like walking without being able to bend the knees. By this time in basic, we were starting to get a little gung ho and had group pride. There were a few in our platoon that weren't as strong as the rest and started to weaken, so in order to have us finish as a group some carried the weaker ones' rifles and urged them along verbally. When we slowed down to a normal pace, walking damn near became enjoyable. If you are wondering if I was a carrier or got carried, the answer is neither; I was just a stiff-legged, keep-moving observer.

The other memorable basic training hike was in the middle of a blizzard. Yes, the northern part of Texas does experience snowstorms. They yelled us awake earlier than normal one morning, "FALL OUT with full field gear and overcoats!" I know it was an earlier than normal reveille, so I'll guess five AM. Before everyone was even in formation, we turned and were moving forward in a column of twos. No one knew what was coming down, as usual. SNAFU.

*Reference note: For the uninitiated, SNAFU in Army parlance means "situation normal, all f***** up." Note that the missing letters also spell "fouled." The other descriptive acronym used was SUSFU, translated "situation unchanged, still f***** up."*

We didn't know it, but storm and blizzard warnings must have been issued. Once out of camp and into the open fields and roads, we knew what we were into. The side winds and blowing snow were so severe that we had to get off the road and lie flat in the ditches to take our breaks. The temperature was down to the point that the water in our canteens froze even though it was sloshed around as we walked. The plan was for us to hike eight miles out to a particular area in a field. Once there, we would go through some kind of field problems or maneuvers. When we arrived we were in knee-deep snow and the sun had come out. After standing around a bit (we couldn't sit as it was too damn cold), the medical people declared it was too cold for the troops to be in the field. How about that? Even for the Infantry! In combat there was no such thing as "too cold," but in combat we did get to dig a hole to get into.

They promptly marched us back to camp. It was now just before noon. We had done 16 miles and had yet to eat. They decided that since we were supposed to be on field rations that day, our lunch would consist of a bowl of soup, a chocolate "D" bar, and coffee. Again, no pampered troops this day. A "D" bar was a vitamin-enriched 600 Calorie chocolate concoction that was hard, coarse-grained, semi-sweet, and about three quarters of an inch thick, maybe three inches wide, and four to four and a half inches long. It was an emergency food item. Its color and taste made one think that it had been stored too long, which was a strong possibility. Truth be known, I would guess that since we were supposed to be in the field for the day, the kitchen had been closed. No one expected us to be back, so you might say the kitchen personnel may have been caught with their pots down.

Reference note: Each company area had its own kitchen during basic training.

Please don't get the idea that since it was now about one PM and we had gotten up earlier than normal, hiked sixteen miles and were hungry, that we would sit around and have a snow day. They crowded us into empty unheated barracks, sat us on the floor and we had indoor classes. Not too bad really!

At the end of our thirteen weeks, they told us we had set a new camp record for total distance walked. At the time I couldn't help but think, "I wonder if they tell every class the same thing?" I don't know about the preceding groups, but for sure we had done our share. After our "graduation" party, the cadre (the yellers) no longer yelled at us and started to talk to us like we were ordinary people. A pleasant change indeed!

KP

The only other highlight that I think worthy of mention was one time that I was told that I had KP duty in the officers' mess the following Sunday.

Reference note: KP means "kitchen police." In Army talk, "police" also means to clean (up), as in "police the area," "police the barracks," "police the latrine," etc. Kitchen police cleaned, and I mean cleaned, everything in the kitchen and the eating area of the mess hall, and also served or waited table.

A side issue comes to mind here that I would like to share. While doing KP during basic training, they had a unique way of drying the silverware all at once. After the silverware had been washed by hand, it was then scalded using boiling water, and while still hot was put in a mattress protector that had an opening on one end only. Two guys would then take each end of the bag and by raising and lowering each end alternately, the silverware sloshed back and forth until dry. Cute!

If you had KP, you had to be awakened an hour or two ahead of the rest. To identify yourself to the person who would awaken you, you tied a towel to the foot of your bed. The CQ would use a flashlight to find the proper bed.

Reference note: The guy with the flashlight was on CQ (charge of quarters). He stayed in the company office and was awake all night to take care of any night business, like a hotel desk clerk.

Now, back to the officers' mess: When the KP detail had gathered in the kitchen, the cook said, "We'll eat first and then work, so what would you like to eat? I'll fix you anything you want." How about that! I think we were dumbfounded for a bit. I can't remember exactly what I overfilled on but it was probably fried eggs, made to my liking with all the trimmings of a complete breakfast.

At noon, the officers were served pan-fried steak. A colonel called me over to his table and told me to take his steak and give it to the cook along with the message that it was too tough. Doing so, I expected the cook to sally forth with some real Army expletives. To my surprise he said nothing, picked up a knife, cut a piece off a quarter of beef that was hanging in the fridge, cooked and served it, and told me to check with the colonel to make sure it was OK. We had steaks as well. Now I knew how some of the upper crust lived. By the way, the officers paid for their own chow. The fare was deducted from their monthly check. They also paid for all their own clothing, dry cleaning, and pressing.

Reference note: During basic, all cadres were two stripe corporals, or three stripe sergeants, and then there were lieutenants, who were commissioned officers. The officers were not yellers, as that would be unbecoming of an officer and a gentleman.

It would only be fair to add here that the training we received was very good, if not great. We were trained to be combat infantry replacements, and I think they did a good job for the most part. That being said, one thing that I think I would have taught the troops is how to use smoke grenades during close-in offensive action. Ordinance would have been required for improving the hand-carried smoke grenades, in order to get more smoke per toss. When a numerically superior laggressive force is moving in on a smaller defensive or delaying force, smoke allows the attacking forces to get nearly on top of the enemy with fewer casualties.

POST-BASIC TRAINING

Paratroops

About three weeks prior to completion of basic training a recruiter from the paratroops gave everyone a sales pitch. One of my buddies was gung ho on that outfit. He became an unappointed recruiter.

I gave in to him and became a volunteer also. Training school for the paratroops was in Fort Benning, Georgia. We knew it was going to be rough, so we did things to get in even better shape as we finished out basic training, like going through the obstacle course twice, the second time voluntarily, etc.

After the train ride to Fort Benning, they separated the group into two halves, as the group was too big for a single class. Separation was done alphabetically. Everyone whose name began with the letters M through Z would have to wait two weeks before starting. The two weeks spent there was, in my estimation, a weeding out period. The food was near criminal and the facilities worse. Now was the time for some loud mouths to be yelling, "You'll be sorry." There were no loud mouths around that place as all were volunteers and all were equally uninformed as to the future. Incidentally, my buddy the unappointed recruiter, whose name was "Lucky" Lockhart from Detroit, Michigan, went through with the first group and I never saw him again, not even during training.

We were right in anticipating that the physical training (PT) would be tough. After the first full day of formal "school" with the calisthenics and running, I was sore. This is a fact: during the evening of the second day of training, I went to the PX (the "post exchange," or the store that sold beer, pop, food, ice cream, cigarettes, etc.). There were three steps up onto a porch at the entrance. I had to use a post, which was on a corner, to help myself up the three steps. I think my body was stiffer than that post and, for sure, more sore.

In paratroop school we learned what discipline and blind obedience really meant. The idea was that you wanted to make it look like you were happy to receive that order, regardless of what the order was, and a prompt and clear reply of "Yes, sir" helped. We were trained how to pack a parachute, how to land on the ground, how to climb a rope, how to hang from a rope with next to no effort, how to exit an airplane, how to steer the direction you were falling as you parachuted to the ground and how to jump from a "mock" tower. The rope training was in case you landed in a tree and you and had to use a rope to shinny up or down.

The mock tower was a platform, about ten foot square, with a wood rail around it. The platform was on top of four telephone poles twenty-five to thirty feet high. One side of the platform had a wall with an opening the size of an airplane door. The student was snapped into a parachute harness without a chute. Attached to the harness was a wide strap, maybe eight to ten feet long, with a snap hook on the end. Running past the side of the tower, parallel to the door side, was a steel cable. Standing in the doorway and facing out, the cable was just above door height, slanting down to the left and upward to the right. The right end of the cable was anchored to a taller telephone pole and the left end to a short pole. Near the short pole, and under the cable was a high pile of dirt. The instructor would help strap you in the harness. The strap coming from the harness had a snap hook on the end, as I said earlier, and the snap hook was snapped to the cable outside the doorway. The trainee would then jump out the door making all the previously instructed proper moves. The slack in the cable would act as a spring and you would slide down the sloped cable and stop at the pile of dirt and then unstrap the harness. Someone would run the harness back to the tower using a tether rope.

When you jumped, you had knees bent, arms crisscrossed across chest, jumping forward while making a quarter turn to the left and yelling "one thousand one, one thousand two, one thousand three." Simple! The hang-up for most was the height factor from the tower. For some, this non-associative fear is not something that can be controlled by the mind.

Reference note: During a live jump, if you get to one thousand three and your main chute hasn't automatically opened, you pull the ripcord on your reserve chute, manually. The main chute was on the jumper's back and the reserve chute was located on the chest. The main chute is opened automatically by a ten foot long strap called a static line that ran from the back of the chute to a cable in the jump plane.

One time, the guy ahead of me was an example of a real acrophobe. He got in the doorway, strapped up of course, and when the instructor said "one, two, three, go," accompanied by a slap on the butt, he hunched but didn't go. "Once again now ..." but no go. "OK, again ..." This time the instructor gave him a good push with his knee and hand. What I didn't mention before was that the jumper was supposed to put his hands on the outside of the doorframe as if to pull with the arms when jumping. The student had put his left hand on the inside of the doorframe. His left foot pivoted and left hand held. There he was, spread-eagled out the door and holding on. It didn't take the instructor long to pull the guy's left hand clear and let him drop and slide. That guy quit the paratroops at the same time I did.

While that guy was going through his trials, a second instructor started talking to me, to occupy my attention, probably. He asked if I was OK and I said yes. He then bet me twenty-five push-ups that I couldn't make a perfect jump. When all of the class had jumped and we were ready to move out that instructor said, "Hey Red [I had dark red hair then], you want me to do those push-ups now?" Of course, I replied, "Yes, sir." Having gotten an instructor to do push-ups for me made me a hero for a day. Every instructor was a three-stripe buck sergeant, and they didn't yell, but at the same time you had better damn well hear, react, and obey. It was a standing rule that any student, for whatever reason, could challenge an instructor to a bare knuckle fight after hours at some place behind the barracks. All officers, regardless of rank were treated the same as the rest of the students during training hours and had to say "sir" to the instructors, instead of vice versa. I witnessed a lieutenant, who had infracted a rule, being reprimanded and told to do twenty-five push-ups (a standard penalty). The officer told the instructor that he had not been wrong and "You will address me as 'sir.'" The instructor, "You're wrong, and make that fifty push-ups." The looie said something else, directed at no one, and the instructor in a firm and threatening voice said, "That will be seventy-five." There were no problems with the instructors as long as you did exactly as they said, promptly and obediently.

Chasing Prisoners

The paratroop school went overboard on discipline and was rough physically. I got to the point where I said, "Who needs this?" Others were quitting so I said "why not?" When it came time to sign the quit slips, some sergeant gave the group a real Army style verbal going over. He must have really worked on his expletives as they were many and raw. His scalding verbiage raked us over like we were Hitler's own children. If swearing gets one to hell, like young mothers tell their children it does, that sergeant will be down in hell along with the big three: Hitler, Stalin, and Mussolini. And should that three striper sit in and play poker with the big three, he will increase the heat with that mule skinner's mouth* of his!

After that little session, we were moved to another area and assigned the principle duty of chasing prisoners. In the Army, a prison was called a stockade. It may be called camp stockade or simply stockade, and the prisoners were all military personnel. Actually, they were holding us, the dropouts, in groups until the groups were large enough to move us to an overseas infantry replacement camp that was ready to handle us.

The food in this new area was worse yet, and one day I had the pleasure of eating in the camp stockade. It was a new experience and my curiosity made me happy to do it. The prison was a large one. Eating utensils consisted of a large spoon and a tin plate. The food was lousy, bordering on terrible: watered down, mushy and without flavor. Lesson: Watch that curiosity.

I'm sure there were some prisoners up for the death penalty, but we were not exposed to them. We handled anything from life sentences down to those still awaiting trial. We referred to this duty as "chasing prisoners." What that entailed was

---

*Back in the days of the old Wild West, a man that drove a wagon pulled by two or up to twenty mules, for pay, was called a mule skinner. They were known for their harsh, raw, unending line of curse words as they pushed, prodded, and drove the mules into pulling what were sometimes tremendous loads.

taking two prisoners out at about 7:30 AM and working them until noon, and then doing the same again in the afternoon. We were issued a rifle or a shotgun with 2 shells or bullets. The final word was if either or both of your prisoners escape, you served their time. Now isn't that sweet? "If you kill a prisoner in an attempted escape, you will be given a military court-martial [a court trial], a carton of cigarettes, and fined one dollar." Simple, but the sad part was that they were dead serious, and the word "dead" wasn't flippantly chosen here, as you will see.

The work the prisoners did, always in pairs, was to sweep streets, rake, and clean up anywhere inside Fort Benning, and also to work the camp dump for salvageable materials. I think I chased prisoners for about three weeks.

There was one particular prisoner that I was assigned to about four times. He called me "GI." More like, "Well f***, we got GI again today." Our directions were that if the prisoners acted up in any way, gave you a bad time, or refused to work, we would just walk them back to the stockade, turn them in, and say that they refused to work. It meant solitary confinement on bread and water rations for ten to 14 days. That particular prisoner tried to push the limits when it came to mouthing off and playing around. When I thought that I had had enough, I would tell him that he had a choice, "Work or walk back, what will it be?" That always quieted him down.

About a half block from the camp dump, there was a building with a bathroom in it. The bathroom was a long room with a toilet at one end and a door at the opposite end. The door leading into the bath had a window that opened to the outside of the building. One day I was chasing a couple of guys at the dump and they asked to go to the can. OK. When we got there, they both went in the john and closed the door. I stood on the outside a minute and thought, hell they can exit the window and just leave me standing here. I kicked open the door and told them to leave it open. Still being a GI.

The day before I left camp, I was going past a bunch of GIs loading onto a Greyhound bus. One guy yelled at me and I walked over. He asked if I remembered him. Looking harder I said, "Sure, you were in the stockade." He said, "Right." Then he told me that he wanted to thank me for guarding him so closely. The day I banged open the bathroom door, he and his buddy had been intending to go out the window. He told me that he had been awaiting trial while in the stockade and that he had been facing a possible fourteen year sentence. The reason that he was out now was that his company commander had gone to bat for him, and now he was headed back to his old group. You never know!

Another time, two prisoners managed to get their guard's gun from him. They told him to walk away. They promptly shot him in the back of the head. One dead guard. The two were captured later and their story and interview appeared in the camp newspaper. Part of their story concerned how they were going to escape from a different guard. They decided not him, because he treated them to donuts at the PX and gave them cigarettes during their breaks. The guy that treated them to doughnuts, etc., was that same guy that had the rough time jumping from the "mock tower." Again, you never know!

The time I was most scared, while chasing prisoners, was on a Sunday when I was called on to do special duty. A group of prisoners had to be taken from the stockade to the camp hospital for sick call. Transportation was a one-ton panel truck ambulance, with Red Cross emblems on the side. The driver was up front with a screen behind him, behind which were six to eight prisoners on long seats that lined the sides. I was in with the prisoners sitting closest to the back door. I was issued an Army .45 for the trip. They could have mobbed me easily. What a setup!

Embarkation

The next step for me, career-wise, was travel orders to report to a port of embarkation. I received a "delay in route" that allowed me to go home for a week before going on to the East Coast. Had I not volunteered for the paratroops, I would have gone to the West Coast and the Pacific Theater of Operations.

The only thing I remember about being home for that week was scaring poor brother Mike (No. 12), age two at the time, by putting on the gas mask that I had in my duffel bag. The only one that could quiet him down at the time was Mom. Additionally, none of my regular buddies were at home, as they were all in service.

At this point, my associates and I at the POE (point of embarkation) were nothing more than infantry replacements. While there, I recall three things that happened. One, we were served some contaminated macaroni and cheese. Everyone had the scoots, runs, or what we called the GIs (this time meaning diarrhea). The big problem was fanning out and trying to find a bathroom, anywhere, that didn't have a line at it. And of course, time was an important factor.

The second memory happened on a Sunday evening. The barracks all had double bunks. I was in the top bunk when I looked toward the door and there stood an officer. I don't know how long he had been standing there, but with one move I was headed for the floor yelling, "Tens hut!" (attention). I landed on the floor in the attention position. As I said, I don't know how long he had been standing there, but I do know from the expression on his face that he wasn't about to do an "about face" (turn 180 degrees) and leave. He walked around the barracks, and asked each man how long he had been in the Army. Memory says the answers were from three months to three years. After his scowling survey he picked out a work detail, and I was part of it. We walked to the train station and unloaded boxes from railroad cars all night, fifty minutes on, ten off, until early morning. We never knew what those boxes contained, except that they were cardboard boxes, big and light. Then back to the barracks and on with the next day, as though nothing had happened. Never saw that "shavetail" (lieutenant) again.

Memory three: We were allowed a pass into New York for the weekend. I went in on a Saturday and was back on a Sunday, so in truth it was an overnighter or a 48 hr. pass. I knew no one in the barracks so I went alone. Downtown Manhattan! So this is Times Square, the place with the moving alphanumeric news and it goes around the corner, just like I had seen in the movies. Second thought: What the hell is so great about that? The thing that amazed me was the crowd of people walking around at night. The sidewalks couldn't hold them and they were over-flowing into the streets. I kept walking and gawking, looking for something that would interest me. I walked, then sat, and walked again, the whole night. Sunday morning came around and I checked the time of the masses at St. Patrick's Cathedral. Now this place I had heard about. Monsignor Fulton Sheen was the name that I saw as being the author on all those pamphlets in the back of the church at home, and here he was. I went in and marveled at the ushers standing around in the back of the church wearing tuxedos. I had heard about that somewhere. If I remember correctly, they charged twenty-five cents per person. Cover charge?

I'm quite sure Monseigneur Sheen started the Mass and I was looking forward to the sermon, as I had heard he was a great talker. I was sitting too far back to make a positive identifica-tion. Anyway I'll never know because I slept through it. There is nothing like the serenity of a church after a full night's walk to put one to sleep.

My next area of attraction was Rockefeller Center. I walked in the main entrance and a young woman in a tour guide uniform was talking to a group. I stopped at the back of the group and listened. It wasn't long before I heard that guide bitch say, "Would the soldier at the back of the group please disassociate himself from the tour?" OK, that was enough. ...Let's find the way back to camp. The friendliness of the big city was just too overwhelming.

ATLANTIC CRUISE

At Sea

I don't remember the exact date of our departure. It took us approximately two weeks to make the crossing. If we landed the night of May 15, 1944 and disembarked on May 16, then we must have loaded and left about May 1st or 2nd. It was an English-owned ship, manned by a British and Australian crew. We traveled in a large convoy of ships. It must have taken a lot of planning and scheduling to organize that whole convoy. The Nazi U-boats were still active in the Atlantic. At all times, lookouts were posted on the periphery of the ship. Troop ships were priority targets as they gave the highest payback per torpedo. The Navy used the troops they were transporting to stand watch for enemy submarines or torpedos. Each person on watch stood on deck and scanned the water by eye, looking for some irregular shape or movement.

The British food aboard ship was tasteless and terrible. After we stopped throwing up from being seasick, the next hurdle was to swallow the food. Let me digress for a moment to stateside and the food. In the States, there were a few things I didn't like. Eggplant for one, shredded beef in a white thick gravy, served on toast, for two. The Army name for number two was "shit on a shingle" and it was served mostly for breakfast. The third thing that never made me feel like writing home about it were carrots, rough-cut, cooked, and served in a white sauce. Yuck! Number four in the listing, but number one on the all-time hate list, and the worst by a wide margin, was mutton stew. The coldest and greasiest was served in Fort Benning. The smell of the sheep never left the meat. Every time I tried it, I could never get past the first mouthful. The kids of today have a very appropriate mime that aptly describes the situation. With mouth wide open and tongue extended, two fingers are placed on the tongue, while the person bends forward and down. Pukesville!

Remember, I was an eighteen year old with a healthy outdoor appetite. Not only that, having grown up in a large family of mostly boys, anytime you showed a reluctance to eat, the sibling sitting on either side of you, or in front for that matter, was happy to help you out. There were no "leaves" (leftovers).

Now back to the ship ...

In the Army, if you have KP and something is left unclean, you are gigged. If gigged, as a penalty you are restricted to the base, you aren't allowed a pass to town, and sometimes you are given more KP duty. On a scale of one to ten, with ten being the best, the kitchen fare on our British ship would rate point eight. As to cleanliness, if those limey kitchens and mess halls followed the above mentioned Army guidelines, those on KP would have had to re-enlist to serve out their restricted time. I for one, survived on boiled potatoes (plain), bread buns, and apricot marmalade. If people who want to diet could only go on those ships! If word spread, Weight Watchers of America would go belly-up.

Being at sea, everything tasted different. It's the salty sea air that does it. Cigarettes tasted totally different. Then again, there are the ship's natural smells and, not to be unexpected, a sprinkling of vomit.

The ship was crowded, so a lot of the guys tried to stay on deck as much as possible. The bathrooms were especially strong in sea salt smell. The showers, urinals, toilets, and washbasins were always wet due to humidity and the fact they were washed down using large water hoses and ocean water.

We disembarked our gourmet pleasure cruise in Liverpool, England and boarded a troop train. The passenger cars were different from what we had seen in the United States. We boarded the cars by way of a line of doors on the side, rather than an entrance on each end. The cars were shorter, more windows and compartmentalized. The train whistle was high pitched and the train had good acceleration and speed. Very different: hey, all right!

When the time came to be fed (now get this!), they passed out a K-ration to each of us. This was a preview of coming attractions. When we got to France we would live—I'll take that word back and say exist—on K-rations for months on end. I would say that for all the time in combat, we ate them eighty to ninety percent of the time. You kind of get to know what a dog feels like eating the same food every day. I'm not joking, for us it was the same rations for months on end.

Rations

As long as we are on the train with nothing to do, I'll tell you about the contents of the rations. The K-ration came in three kinds: breakfast, dinner, and supper. All three rations came in individual boxes. The boxes were a little thicker than a box of Cracker Jack and about the same size, length- and width-wise. Each box had double cardboard outer layers. The outermost was a thin pulpy cardboard, like cardboard on the back of an 8 1/2" x

11" paper pad, but half as thick. The inner cardboard was a more solid cardboard and was impregnated with a generous amount of wax. The wax understandably made the box waterproof. That worked well, but the best and most useful aspect of the waxed box was that in combat we split the end open, poured out the contents, stood the box on end, and lit the top (the opened end) with a match. It burned like a candle. It lasted long enough to heat a canteen cup half full of water. It was also useful to start a small twig fire for some serious water heating. By serious, I mean a full canteen cup or a stew from a raw vegetable we might come across in a field along the way.

There were changes made in some of the contents of the different K-rations. During my sojourn in Europe, they were practically always as described here. All three K-rations, i.e., breakfast, dinner, and supper, when added together contained 3,000 Calories. The boxes contained absolutely no printing on the outside other than the word breakfast, dinner or supper. The government, in the interest of security, specified it this way.

Now for the contents. A can, a little smaller than a tuna fish can, was the main course. For breakfast, it was packed with scrambled eggs, somewhat the consistency of bulk tofu. Lunch was processed American cheese plain, or for variety, some had bacon added to the cheese. The bacon was the size of flyspecks and added more color than flavor. Oh, how I would grow to hate the repetition ... that goddamn packy, stick-to-the-roof-of-your-mouth, flat-tasting, bowel-binding, pile-aggravating, processed American cheese, that made us poop like rabbits. I'm glad the thought of that cheese doesn't upset me—if I think of it long at all, I'm sure I'll have an impaction.

The supper ration had a kind of beef pâté that was like a meat loaf using triple ground hamburger, in the same size of can as the other two.

The powdered drink envelopes, one in each ration, contained instant coffee for breakfast, orange or lemon drink for lunch, and bouillon for evening dining. The instant orange/lemon was fortified with vitamin K to help you clot faster if you bled, like having your hemorrhoids heal faster to handle the next day's cheese. That dietitian took care of us, coming and going.

If instant bouillon powder could grow bouillon trees, Europe would be a solid, no space available, forest today. The Europeans should thank God each day that that stuff was environmentally safe. The only time we used it was to flavor something we stole and stewed from a field. It wasn't even compatible, flavor-wise, with that damn cheese.

Each ration had crackers to go with the entrée, four crackers that contained ingredients that made them much more substantial health-wise. The four crackers together were the size of two soda crackers. We never really got tired of them, unlike that damn cheese.

I remember now that brother Lynn told me one time he got along OK with the cheese. According to him, it didn't affect his morning regularity and he kind of liked the smoothness and flavor. (Well I'll be!) I remember another thing having to do with Lynn and cheese. When I was in about fourth grade (which would put Lynn in the sixth grade), Lynn found a box of cheese in the road. The box was just lying there in the road and curiosity got the better of him. I don't know if he gave it a kick first, probably did, and found it was heavy. He hauled it home and after opening it, discovered it full of one pound packages of cheese. We always said that Lynn was the "lucky one" in the family. The cheese didn't last very long as there were ten mouths at home at the time, and of course the Depression was on.

In the K-rations, each one of the meal cans had a key for an opener. The can had a tab that you would peel away from the side using your thumbnail. You would insert the tab through the slit or eye of the key and start twisting the key. The metal strip, as it was removed from the can, wound around the stem or shaft of the key. There must be a million of the remains of those, as well as the cans, in the ground in Europe. They now have bouillon-flavored soil rich in tin.

Many times we would open the cheese can an inch or so and then hold the can over a fire until the cheese started oozing out, for melted cheese and crackers. If we came across a field of onions we requisitioned them, as they worked well with cheese. Apple trees, pear trees, plum trees, grapes, carrots, potatoes, and even white turnips were all fair game as we walked past or through. How about saying it was "fair fare?"

Many a GI got the "GIs" from eating too much green fruit at once. Not to worry. There were no latrine lines when you lived in the field, and we were well versed in digging holes. Additionally, every ration had a small packet of toilet paper. We always carried a reserve supply of paper inside our helmet making it conveniently handy. It was always dry and it added a degree of class to being in the field: when we went to the bathroom we always removed our helmets.

Every ration had four cigarettes, a book of matches containing eight matches, the above-mentioned toilet paper, and a stick of gum. The cigarettes were all the popular brands of the day and just about everyone smoked. Cigarettes sold for five cents a pack overseas. Since we were in no position to shop, they were furnished to us for free. Note: I can't help but wonder if the government has made sure all K-rations have been destroyed on account of media coverage and the cigarette guilt-trip placed on those that smoke.

How could I forget dessert? Breakfast was a raisin fig bar, half the size of a Milky Way candy bar. Dinner was a piece of fortified chocolate that tasted like chalk mixed with water with a touch of chocolate flavoring added, same size as the raisin fig bar. Supper was a mixed fruit bar, the same size again. I forgot, for all of the above you furnished your own water. Now that doesn't sound too bad, does it? The hitch is living on them for months on end.

I have since read an article about the man who invented the K-rations. He said they were designed for emergency conditions to stop a person from starving. The Army tried them and decided that with a little persuasion, they could be made to go much further and longer. Pity, again.

Every now and then, we got a C-ration. There were no designated meal types on them. They all came in cans, about the size of one half a Campbell soup can. I don't remember all the varieties of these, but those I do remember are beans & Vienna sausage, noodles with slivers of small brown pieces (beef), and beef hash. Word was that the same rations were served in WWI. They didn't taste that old, really. I recall one time, sitting on the side of a freshly dug fox hole and eating a can of hash. Along came an emaciated, ribs-sticking-out, underfed dog. Liking dogs and feeling sorry for him, I offered him my can of half-eaten hash. He stuck his nose in the can, smelled it, and walked away. I told him I didn't blame him and ate the rest anyhow.

The biscuits, toilet paper, matches, and salt/baking soda came in another type of can. I don't recall if there were cigarettes, but there probably were. Now, those biscuits were something else: four of them, one quarter inch thick, round, and just smaller than the inside diameter of the can. No one had enough of a disregard for his teeth to try and bite through them. Hard? Man, you don't know what hard is! I'll bet a hockey puck, frozen or otherwise, is softer. The idea was to grip them with your back teeth while pushing up with the heel of your hand. Make 'em snap. The flavor wasn't bad and they helped develop the neck and jaw muscles. A scrape on the cheek now and then was tolerable, as the dirt and facial stubble acted as a buffer.

The salt/baking soda that was part of the ration came in a small tube about the size of a mechanical pencil lead container. Its intended use was as toothbrush powder (and if you lacked a brush, you used your index finger). Once again, you supplied your own water, or were rewarded with a long aftertaste. One of the cutest field expedients I heard of was an alternate use of the salt/baking soda. Recipe: soak C-ration biscuits or crackers in water, until mushy. Add salt/baking soda. Mix and let rise. Pour on skillet and make pancakes. Instead of "add salt to the desired taste while mixing," "add biscuits until the salt taste has been suppressed."

The rations we liked far and above the rest were called 10-in-1s. The name derived from the fact that there was enough to feed ten men in one box. Once again, I don't know all the ingredients; we were never issued them. The ones we did get were begged, mostly from tankers. The tankers had the wherewithal to haul around boxes. A five-man crew manned a medium-sized tank. With 10-in-1s, each box had enough for two meals.

The 10-in-1 ingredients I do remember were canned (cooked) scrambled eggs with enough ham that a person could actually taste it. The can was about the size of a large tomato can, approximately one pound. Bacon was another ingredient I remember: regular raw strip bacon, in a can about the size of a standard can of salmon. Now, you say, what can a dogface do with raw bacon in the field with nothing to cook with? Fear not, there is a way! We did it by opening both ends of the can and pushing the strips out. The can was packed laying the strip bacon out, piece overlapping piece, on a long full-length strip of paper. Then the paper was rolled until the round bundle matched the inside size of the round can. Then, I'm sure, the bundle was just pushed in the can. Tucked in this way, it was easy for us to remove the ends and push the bacon out.

We then slit the can top to bottom, folded it flat, and bent up the edges. Four rocks placed in a square around a small fire, made a proper support for the bacon pan. What a treat! The 10-in-1s also had jam and real butter.

We had a hot meal very infrequently: Christmas and Thanksgiving for sure, and maybe three or four times additionally. I recall that one time while on line, the kitchen got some hot food to us. What the menu consisted of has passed from my memory, but I do remember the white bread. The bread was such a treat that we didn't eat it but saved it. To protect and preserve it, each of us carried our one thick slice of bread inside our shirts and down by the belt line, I made my one slice last two days.

I'm glad the train stopped long enough for me to cover field rations. … Onward!

Tent City

We wound up in an abandoned orphanage that night. There were double bunks and the top bunk was about thirty inches off the floor. The bottom bunk was just shy of the floor. There must have been small kids sleeping there ahead of us. The British took most of their children to the country to avoid the bombings and it is probable that this orphanage was empty for that reason.

The next day was disappointingly uneventful. Being May 17, and my 19th birthday, I thought the Queen would show up. She had not made it to the docking of the boat, so naturally I figured she had saved her visit for my birthday. But she didn't show, nor did her sister Margaret. Didn't they realize that infantry replacement, presently unassigned to any division, Private R. McDonnell was there to help protect the British throne, and all her colonies? Hear, hear! I made a mental note to make appropriate changes in my social calendar, after all I was now nineteen, and those kinds of things certainly had to be noted.

We moved from the orphanage to an Army installation that could be called a "tent city." We were in the field and it was a veritable sea of tents, eight or ten men to a tent, and folding Army cots to sleep on. The trick about sleeping on an Army cot was to put as much under you as on top. Nights were cold even in May. In addition to the two standard Army blankets, we used newspapers under the blankets and spare clothes from our duffel bags for more warmth on top. Where there's a will, there's a way, especially if one is cold.

The Army always tried to keep the troops busy. Sunday morning was a good time to police the area. When you policed, the group formed a line shoulder-to-shoulder, moved forward, and picked up anything on the ground that was not growing. A command was yelled, and kept short: "ALL RIGHT EVERYBODY, MOVE FORWARD, AND IF IT'S NOT GROWING PICK IT UP! I DON'T WANT TO SEE ANYTHING BUT ELBOWS AND ASSHOLES!" We were picking up as ordered when I heard someone yell, "Hey, Bob." Turning, I was surprised and delighted to see brother Ed.

Ed had been visiting the Red Cross in the nearby town of Warminster, in western England. He read through the guest register and spotted my name. Wonderful! I got permission to leave the camp for the rest of the day. We went into Warminster, a small town really, and as there were no pubs open, we browsed around talking and eating at the NAFFI (Navy, Army, and Air Force Institutes), which was like an American Red Cross or USO. Some of the NAFFIs in England were like hotels with rooms to let and were very economical. Unlike our Red Cross units, they didn't serve fried cakes; they served crumpets. Crumpets were small crackers, cookies, and small cakes which weren't too sweet, sugar being high on the ration list. The small villages in England were not very exciting on a Sunday afternoon, but surprisingly, even the small villages had uniformed bands that marched and played around their main street each Sunday. It would have been interesting to learn the history of the uniforms they wore. No matter, Ed and I enjoyed being together and talking about our Army lives thus far, and about the different bits of news from our family.

The food in tent city was middle-of-the-road. We dined using our metal mess gear while being served cafeteria style, out-of-doors. Eating outside, there was plenty of available seating. We all know that it rains a bit in merry old England. Have you ever gone through a cafeteria-style food line in the rain? It's different, and just in case you try it, I'll give you a tip: it's better to pour the water off of your food before eating! The benefit to being outdoors is that it doesn't matter where you pour that excess water! Another tip: A fork works better than a large spoon, but only if the food tastes better than the rain. There was a positive side to this, though: the mess gear washed easier! The weather in England is so, er, ah, ...refreshing.

HEY, WHAT'S THAT NOISE?

The wake up call we had that morning was neither a bugle nor someone sticking their head in the tent yelling, "OK, up and at 'em!" but the roar of what must have been hundreds of airplane engines filling the damp morning air. Bypassing our clothes, we scrambled out of the tents to look at the "visibility unlimited sky," and what a sight it was. Wave after wave of airplanes filled the sky as they straggled and limped on their way back from their early morning missions. In kind of hushed tones, word spread among those of us on the ground, "The invasion is on."

The neat pattern of planes flying in formation was gone, being replaced by what appeared to be groups just trying to get back to their bases. They were like wounded soldiers returning from battle, totally fatigued and in disarray. As I said, the sky just seemed to be filled with them. Airplanes had replaced the clouds. Large majestic bombers were most impressive as they churned along, appearing to be flying slower than the others around them. We could see that many were wounded, although from the ground we couldn't see exact detail. Some of those beauties were really flying low. You could see an odd bomber losing altitude, peeling off, and going into a long slow spiral to earth. What a sight that was and what a feeling of awe and admiration mixed with pity and sorrow for those in the planes going down.

The date was June 6, 1944 and the invasion was on. The largest naval force in the history of mankind was hauling personnel and supplies to breach the defenses on the beaches of Normandy. We were hungry for details and any possible news pertaining to the invasion, but when "You're in the Army Now," receiving word on what was going on was not meant-to-be.

I remember they gave us gas mask training on that never-to-be-forgotten historical day. Put on the mask, walk into a small shed with tear gas in it, take off the mask, take a sniff of the gas, and walk out. We were exposed to the gas long enough to appreciate the effectiveness of the gas mask. It's a good thing those gas masks didn't grow when buried. Everyone was issued one for combat. Two to three weeks after being in combat they had all mysteriously disappeared. The bayonet lasted longer but it eventually went the same way as the gas mask.

Meanwhile, as we remained in England, they kept us busy marching up and down the blacktop country roads. They wanted to make sure no one missed out on the free walking tours. I'm sure the real idea was to keep us busy and in shape until the time came to fulfill our mission as infantry replacements.

Reference note: By the time all 156,000 men of the initial landing forces were on French territory, the Allies had lost 11,000 men, killed, wounded, and missing in action. Replacements were vital to keep fighting units up to their TO strength (table of organization or, say, twelve men to each squad, three full squads to a platoon, and on up the line of divisional structure). If you lose 11,000, you need 11,000 to replace them. The replacement depots (Army slang called them "reppo deppos") became critical to the logistics of war.

According to one of the Webster dictionaries, the use of the word "D-Day" was first used in WWI, by the British Army. They took the first letter of the word "day" (D), then added the word "day" to it, and called it "D-Day." D-Day was then used to define the unspecified starting date of any large or momentous military event. Today, anyone using the word or expression D-Day is referring to June 6, 1944, when the largest seaborne military force ever assembled in history was set in motion for the invasion of France.

The title for the overall operation was designated "Operation Overlord." The password for the day was, "Mickey ... Mouse." The troops going in on the beaches had no immediate use for the password but the paratroops that started landing right after 12:01 on June 6, as well as the glider troops landing before daybreak, needed a password. In addition to the password, the paratroopers used a clicker that sounded like a cricket so they could identify each other in the dark without speaking and having the possible enemy know that they were Americans. After D-Day, there was a different password each day as long as we were in combat.

LET'S TAKE A BOAT RIDE

To the best of my recollection, ten to fourteen days after D-Day, they boated us on a short trip across the English Channel. I can't remember what transported us from ship to shore, but I do recall walking inland and then buddying up to dig a hole. Our new sleeping quarters were a step down comparatively. This would not change for some time to come. The music of the night was the distant thunder of artillery, and later, as we joined our appointed divisions, it would become the symphony of the daylight hours as well, and appreciably louder, as you may expect. We had been issued live ammunition. No one ever told us when to load or unload again. From that day on our rifles became part of us, whether we were eating, sleeping, or when we took our helmets off.

I have read in my 79th Infantry Division book, published after the war, where Co. I, 314th Regiment caught hell and suffered a high rate of casualties on their way in to Cherbourg. The same book related how the 79th Division was responsible for the fall of Cherbourg. Cherbourg was a major port city and was the number one objective after the beachhead landing. The Allied forces needed the port and its facilities to get troops and supplies ashore. I was destined to replace one of those who had fallen as a casualty in the second squad, second platoon of Co. I.

When we went on the beach, we carried everything we owned including our full duffle bag. One day, they moved us to a particular area and had us pile all our gear in a heap and told us to get rid of everything that wasn't personal. When we walked away we had shorts, socks, boots, fatigue pants, undershirt, fatigue shirt, fatigue jacket, helmet liner, steel helmet, belt, ammo belt, eating utensils, M1 rifle, 8 clips of ammunition (8 rounds to the clip), canteen, first aid pack, gas mask, bayonet, and anything loose that happened to be in our pockets. Oops, I forgot: an entrenching tool, which was almost as important as our pants, and a raincoat or poncho. The poncho was more versatile and worked better all around than the raincoat, while at the same time both of them sweat on the inside as we walked in the rain on a warm day. The poncho fit over everything we wore and came off fast and easy. It would also cover the M1 when it was slung upside down while walking in the rain. During the rain, or snow for that matter, the poncho covered the hole we slept in better than a raincoat. When we weren't using the poncho (and/ or raincoat), it was folded and draped over our ammo belt and carried in the middle of the back.

We didn't know it, but we were now attired with our summer outfit that we would wear until I can't remember when. I'm sure we went several months, if not longer. We managed to stay aired out to some extent, since we were outside all the time—even when it was raining. Mother Nature and the good Earth substituted for washer and dry cleaner, and all overlooked the lack of creases in our pants. Being one with nature, muddy boots were common and, come to think of it, when the bottom of our holes became muddy, mud on any other part of our attire was not uncommon either. Mud wasn't bad, wet was uncomfortable, and later on, frozen wet was most uncomfortable.

HEY, WHAT'S UP, DOC?

When it came to being informed on what, where, when, and how, I can sum it up very easily: we weren't. With very rare exception were we ever told a thing. The standard was, "saddle up & move out," or "stop, spread out, and dig in." We had no news other than rumors, and I'm talking about the entire time we were in combat. We were trained to take orders in blind obedience, and that was the way it was.

In combat, we carried an additional bandolier of ammo and some grenades from time to time. A bandolier was a cotton cloth container that had eight side-by-side pockets. Each pocket contained one clip of .30 caliber ammunition. One half of the bandolier's length was a one-half inch wide cloth. The circular bandolier was slung over the head and under one arm. The ammunition side was carried in front and across the chest. It went off and on easily and was in a position that made it easy to carry.

The grenades we might carry were the standard high explosive shrapnel type. They look like a small pineapple. Some guys also carried a grenade launcher adapter, which was a device that slid right over the end of an M1 rifle. The grenade had an adapter that slid over said rifle attachment. A blank shell was used to launch or fire it. When firing a grenade launcher, the butt of the rifle was placed on the ground or it could be fired from the shoulder. If the shoulder was used, it was best to hold it firmly against the shoulder and lean into it. The kick was decent. The different grenades available for a rifle launcher were HE (high explosive, fragmented), antitank, smoke, and white phosphorous. Phosphorous started burning when exposed to air, and kept burning until it died out. The laws of physics didn't change if it landed on you or the next guy. It burned in you until it burned itself out. We were told our defense was to knock it off the skin as fast as possible, or to try and cover it with mud to cut off the oxygen. The Germans never used the grenade launcher that I know of. Our artillery and infantrymen did, especially when fighting house-to-house. The rifle launcher was used when we needed to throw at a distance, as it threw further than what we could throw by hand.

NO LONGER A REPLACEMENT

Getting Started

Yeah! We, my fellow replacements and I, joined our battle-weary brethren, around K-ration time (for supper). We were advised of the uncertain future and were told when in doubt as to what to do, just pick a vet and follow him. That was some of the best advice I ever got, and later I gave the same advice. If he hits the ground, you hit the ground. When he stands up, you stand up. When he moves, you move. When he tries to get his butt below grass height, you do the same.

We were also told that the vets were weary and tired, so we would pull guard duty for the night. We wanted to ask, in the interest of a little guidance: Where are we? Are there Germans around here? Have you been attacked at night? What do you look for? Who do we get a hold of? We were placed by twos around the perimeter, and my buddy and I were assigned a spot in a gully. As far as directions went, we were told, "don't talk, keep your ears open, don't fall asleep, and don't f*** up." "One quick question, sir, when will we be relieved?" Answer, "shut up and you'll find out."

It was a scary night.

It didn't take long until our eating utensils boiled down to one tablespoon, which was carried in a jacket pocket, boot, or anywhere else. The canteen cup was indispensable. The canteen slipped into the cup contour precisely and the two of them were carried inside a canvas carrier bag. The bag had snaps on top and a wire hook arrangement that mated with holes on our ammo belts. Canteen and cup were contoured on one side to fit the contour of the hip. We usually carried it on the right hip and a little to the rear. The canteen, when full, jumped on the hip when we had to run, but that was better than having it empty.

The Bocage

When we moved out the next day, we followed in line. We were in the Normandy hedgerows now. The French called this area the "bocage." The fields were all divided into squares up to a city block square. The field dividers were a continuous mound of dirt up to six feet high and maybe five to eight feet thick at the base. The mound was made up of dirt, stone, weeds, vines, and bushes all the way up to the size of small trees. Every field had a wagon width gate in one corner and another wagon width gate on one of the other three hedgerows. The gates allowed the farmer to go into one field and out into the next and isolate their animals field by field. Every so often there was a lane running through in a relative straight line for maybe an acre, or out to the limit of a farmer's land. The lane was wide enough for a wagon or a medium-sized tank. Some of the lanes were almost covered on top by vines, tree branches, and wild growth. Oh, that maudit (French for "damnable") bocage!

90

It was the perfect natural defense terrain for the Germans, or as the French called them, "les Bosch." The Bosch dug in and through the hedgerow until they had a two or three inch hole to shoot through. It was nearly impossible for us to see the hole due to distance and density of the overgrowth. At times, the Germans and Americans would be on opposite sides of the same hedge–now it became grenade time.

Below is a picture of what a hedgerow looked like, as of 1982. The lane down the center, depending on its width, was used militarily for different purposes. The Germans moved their personnel back and forth, in wagons or jeeps, and sometimes, if wide enough, a tank was moved through. Notice the gate on the right side of the picture. There is probably a gate on the left, but out of sight. The gates would open to fields where farmers planted their crops or where their animals grazed. The picture gives good insight as to what the overgrowth around the fields looks like. There is corn growing in the field on the right.

Figure 1. Hedgerow in 1982

I will refer back to the hedgerows from time to time as this narrative unfolds, so please be patient with this old dogface as I run you around the country first and then back to the hedgerows.

"HI, DOC" AND SNIPERS

Captain Goldberg

When we moved from point to point in the bocage, we always traveled single file. Like I said, we never knew where we were or where in hell we were going. When the line stopped, we stopped. Usually there was some kind of small arms fire going on around us, so whenever we stopped, we laid flat. One day we were in such a position and this medic came walking through like he was on Broadway and just enjoying the hell out of the weather. He wore the Red Cross armband and a red cross with white background on his helmet. He spoke to every guy who looked at him. I learned he was an MD and a captain and was unintentionally building quite a reputation. He drove around on a jeep along with a couple of guys who were litter bearers. He didn't stay back at battalion aid and wait for the wounded to be brought to him. Instead, he went around finding the wounded, going into situations where the brave would not tread. Talk about getting in harm's way! He would ride his jeep under shell fire, get out and yell at the litter bearers to get out of the jeep and get this wounded guy or that one. His name was something like Goldberg. (Captain Goldberg, sorry sir!)

The story goes that one time a sniper was harassing Captain Goldberg and his bunch. They were in the rear, someplace.

Let me interject a word here about snipers. A German sniper would hide and allow the "line" of U.S. GIs to pass. He would now be positioned behind our lines. Shooting from a long distance, he would kill all he could. After three days when his food ran out, he'd crawl down or out of hiding and give up. I told myself that if a sniper surrenders to me, he's dead. Ditto for the SS troopers, who were Hitler's own elite troops and usually in charge. Each SS trooper had the letters SS tattooed on his left arm. The SS were also known to head up a bunch of non-German civilians, put them in uniform and into combat with the choice of fighting or being shot on the spot. Fortunately, I never had to make the decision of shooting a sniper or an SS trooper and thus wind up with it on my conscience.

Getting back to Captain Goldberg, he or someone else spotted a sniper who was harassing them one day. The Geneva Conference rules stipulated that medical personnel will not be fired at or on. Captain G. borrowed a knife and went after the sniper. He circled around behind the sniper and came at him from his back. They say he got the sniper. I don't know if the story is true or not. (Medical personnel aren't supposed to kill the enemy either, but they can take action in self-defense.) I do know that we had a lot of respect for him, and each time we saw him out and around we somehow felt better. He was starting to become a legend with us, and incidentally, when I got wounded five months later, I ran into the captain in the hospital area. He too had picked up a piece of shrapnel. After introducing myself, we talked over our respective wounds, shook hands, and departed. I returned to my outfit later but never saw him again. In retrospect, I wish I had asked him, "Off the record, was that sniper story really true?" He was the only MD I ever saw, on line. (The term on line referred to the GIs that were the closest to the Germans). The fact that there were so many GIs, always a minimum of 30 to 40 in a particular area and strung in a line facing Jerry-land, made up that imaginary line. (One of the nicknames for the Germans was Jerry; Jerry-land was German territory.)

Shooting at Me

One day while still in Normandy and in the "maudit" hedgerows, we were strung out in a winding single file line and were temporarily stopped. I was lying there minding my own business, when KA-WHAP. That sound was a bullet hitting the ground near my head. The sniper had picked me out for some reason. I could not evacuate the area so I moved back several guys and lay down again. KA-WHAP again. That S.O.B. had moved with me. You could not see them firing nor hear the rifle, because they fired from great distances. The only thing you heard was the bullet going by your head or when it hit something near. If his aim was good you heard nothing, I guess. Snipers always shot or aimed at the head. The ordinary rifleman aimed at the torso. I moved again and then we all moved. Maybe he shot at someone else the next time the line stopped, you never knew. "... Keep moving. ..."

It happened another time, another day, while I was moving. I knew it had been close by the sound: a slight buzz and ka-whap. The only thing I could do was curse him (as I said earlier, we had our reasons for swearing at times) and keep moving.

Still another time, but this time the Jerry had a burp gun and he was close. It was just turning dark and we were a party of five or six going back to get the next day's supplies of water and K-rations. The field had the usual entrance/exit. The actual gate had a pair of permanent upright posts at each end of the opening and three horizontal rails between the verticals. We were just getting to the gate when that Kraut S.O.B. let out with a blast. This was not a sniper S.O.B., this was an ordinary German soldier S.O.B. You have never seen six guys go through a three rail fence so fast, some over the top, some through the middle, and the rest via the bottom. If we had practiced it for a month, we couldn't have done it any faster. Maybe we surprised him, but he didn't hit any of us. We hung tight for a little and then moved out. Jerry probably moved out faster than we did. He was the one behind enemy lines.

A "burp gun" is a handheld automatic firing machine gun. It fired so fast that the sound made more of a continuous burp sound, rather than a tat-tat-tat sound. Hence the nickname, "burp gun." The Germans used them a lot. Once you heard it, there was no mistaking it. As a matter of fact, after some experience in combat you could tell the difference as to who fired what weapon. We could identify their rifle, our rifle, their machine gun, our machine gun, their airplane in the sky, or our airplane, without looking up. You may think their artillery is to the front and ours to the rear. Right, easy. But experience taught us how far beyond or how close an explosive shell would land, and that was all with respect to the most important piece of ground in the world, the one we were on—or in.

We never really developed a fear of small arms fire. That doesn't mean that we didn't respect it and take immediate and appropriate action. If a bullet hit next to you, buzzed past your ear, clipped a bush or tree limb, no adrenaline flowed. If it hit your helmet, passed through your clothes or hit your canteen, then maybe a little adrenaline, followed by telling your buddies about it. I never had any low flows, but I know of many cases. One of my buddies had a bullet ricochet off his helmet, took a bullet in the canteen, and had an antitank gun shell miss his belt buckle, going from left to right. I'll mention how he died later; his name was Kraff—remember it.

ENEMY ARTILLERY

88s

The thing that put the fear of God, and every other ass-puckering-fear-you-can-think-of into us, was direct fire from high explosive 88 mm guns. The "Churmans" used the 88s very extensively. The muzzle velocity was just below the speed of sound. When it was fired at you, under direct fire, you heard it fire and before you could react, it hit. By direct fire, I mean that those that fire the 88, or any other piece of artillery for that matter, can actually see the target they are firing at. A good example of not having enough time to react would be if you were to hit the table with the flat of your left hand and then hit the table with your right hand, with as little time in between as possible. That is the amount of time between fire and explosion. The further away the gun, the more time between bang … BANG. When they had the high ground it was even more effective. When you hear that distinctive bang … BANG, your first thought as you hit the ground is, "Is there anything I can get behind or is there anything I can get between me and that gun?" If the answer is "no," then you either move or get hit, if you aren't hit already. It takes real will power to get up and run, but you have no other choice. This kind of stuff takes the "a" out of atheist, by the way.

They used the 88 shells on their tanks, on moveable antitank guns, on direct fire field pieces, for long range shelling, and for antiaircraft shelling. It was handy to have the same size shell around. An 88 could, and did, go through both sides of the turret on a small tank. It could knock the turret off of a medium-sized tank. Our tanks, with their 75 mm, feared the 88.

Tanks

Let it be known that a tank had its good points and its bad points. Ideally, tank commanders wanted open ground, so no one and nothing could get near them. The tankers would not go inside a village or in a wooded area unless the infantry was at their side. Tankers would refuse to move into those areas where they might expose themselves to an enemy bazooka, Molotov cocktail, or a six-inch diameter wooden post shoved between the drive wheels and the tank track. (A Molotov cocktail is a whiskey or wine bottle filled with gasoline and a piece of cloth pushed into neck of the bottle, instead of its normal cork stopper. Saturate the rag with gasoline, light it and you now have an effective bomb that if thrown and smashed on the back of the tank can start the tank on fire and knock it out of service.) If a post was shoved between the drive sprocket and tank track, or tread, the tank spun in circles until someone rescued it. If the tanker was stopped with enemy troops around, it was just a matter of time until they were dead or captured. Today's tanks are a totally different story.

If an enemy tank came at us and it was in the open, or with infantry, we gave ground fast. When we were dug in, in a wooded area, and one of our own lumbering noisy tanks moved in near us, we started getting pucker butt. The Germans would hear the tank and know someone was there, so they would send in a little artillery to quiet things down. The tankers didn't care, they just buttoned up, by getting inside and closing all of the openings. It was different for us: the infantry had to move or be dug in.

Reference note: It was possible to lie flat on the ground and have a 105 mm or a 155 mm shell hit three or four feet away from you, and walk away. It comes from the fact that the shell buries itself, a little before exploding. The softer the ground, the deeper it goes. The explosion and shrapnel go up and forward at an angle rather than close and parallel to the ground. If you are on either side of the impact point the explosion may have a tendency to roll or flip you over on the ground. You may even get knocked out or lose your ability to hear for a while, but it is possible to walk away. I know, first hand.

Psychological Effects

There is a psychological effect called conditioned response. In combat we were subjected to some of these conditional responses. Allow me to try and explain this, while bearing in mind that I am just a layman.

In combat, we soon developed a conditioned response to different sounds: the sound of a rifle (theirs or ours?) or a machine gun or a German "burp gun" being fired, the distinct sound of a mortar being fired, airplanes passing over (with the distinct differences between the German and Allied planes). When you heard each different sound, you responded differently. Artillery not only had distinctive sounds, but overall had a cumulative effect on the mind: the sound of the German artillery piece being fired, the sound of the shell as it passed through the air, the mental estimation of where it would hit, the sound of impact with the ground, the sound of impact with a tree, the follow-through of the flying shrapnel after explosion, and the lingering smell of powder. These series of sounds and effects of the artillery instilled a fear in us, a conditioned fear that grew exponentially as soon as we realized the shells were going to hit close in. The fear also grew in your mind the more times you were exposed to it. It could and did make walking zombies out of some. (Incidentally, we never yelled, "Incoming!" as they do in the movies when our ears picked up the sound of an artillery shell. Also, artillery shells do not whistle as they travel through the air.)

If you are in a hole and a 105 mm or 155 mm shell hits within ten feet of you, the sound of it coming in is different. It keeps building up louder and louder until it crescendos to a point that it sounds like the roar of a train. You do have time to evaluate it as to how close it will hit. When a shell comes in on you, if you are in a hole, you already know that the only way it can get you is a direct hit or a hit close enough to cave your hole in on you. In anticipation, you go into the fetal position, helmet on, arms up and folded on each side of your head and legs folded with knees up and under the face. (The overall body position is the same if you are caught above ground and are unable to abandon the area.) Invariably you clench your teeth and tense up completely, but that accomplishes nothing. Oh yeah, don't forget to keep your mouth open to normalize the pressure on your eardrums. If someone is in the hole with you, as there mostly was, you don t have room for the fetal position: you lie side by side, cover the sides of your head with your arms, and say something appropriate after each near miss.

Spotters

Early in the game, the Krauts had their guns (artillery) zeroed in ahead of time on probable targets, crossroads for sure. They would fire a few shells, every now and then, just hoping to hit something. Their long range guns were brought into play on this random firing tactic. Sometimes they left a spotter behind to direct fire for them on any target that showed up. Their artillery spotters always went to the high ground. The ultimate high ground spotter (we used them, not the Germans) was a guy up in a Piper Cub with maps with grid coordinates and a pair of powerful field glasses. The artillery director on the ground had an identical map. They could really zero in fast on any particular target. The results were deadly. If you travel to Europe today ,you will see a lot of churches with missing steeples because the Germans used them for observation posts. The Allies were cautioned not to destroy the churches unless absolutely necessary.

It was fun to watch when a Kraut pursuit plane came over and the American Piper Cub was just lollygagging along. When the Piper pilot spotted the Me 109 or its equivalent, he turned the nose of his plane straight at the ground, dove down, and ran with his wheels six feet off the ground. He did some real hedge-hopping. If the Me missed on the first pass, he was done. He couldn't maneuver against that slow moving low target. The game was deadly, but for us, amusing.

There was another time when we got our ghoulish kicks. Being at the "front," we envied and wanted to share our adventures with those to the rear of us, or "the rear echelon." The Krauts had some long distance low velocity artillery. The large shell traveled so slowly through the air that sometimes you could actually see it going by. The shell had a distinct sound and when we heard it we knew it was headed way back. We made appropriate comments like, "That'll wake up that rear echelon bunch," or "Let's hear it from the boys in the back rows," etc. No respect! Anything in back of our own platoon leader, who usually dug in behind us, was rear echelon.

The worst shelling that I ever experienced on a pure quantity level was one time in the late fall of 1944. We were dug in, in a wooded area. The Krauts thought we were something important and decided to really sock it to us. Thank God they didn't have our exact position. They concentrated on an area about a quarter to half a city block behind us. The next day we moved back and out of that area. In doing so, we went past the area that they had shelled so heavily. The size of the shelled area was about a half of a square city block. Every tree in it was cut off about knee high, but "cut off" is too clean a way of saying it: the trunk stumps were highly erratic and totally splintered. A good analogy would be to say the splinters sticking out the tops of the stump were like the quills of a curled porcupine but not quite as orderly. The limbs were all chopped and splintered and sticking out of the mud like a giant hand had smashed everything and had just kept smashing it. Everything was mud splattered. It was very disconcerting to see Mother Nature so ruined and degraded.

In the winter it was often demoralizing, especially when one's spirits were low, to see an open stretch of a snow covered field, beautifully white, sun shining and then see splotches where shells had hit, throwing black and gray dirt forward from the hole in a fan-shaped pattern.

YOU WANT TO SEE ARTILLERY?

Impressive Artillery

After all is said and done, the German artillery could not compare with ours. Our guns weren't bigger, we just had a lot more of them and didn't hesitate to make them dance in rhythm. When it came to dishing out instant hell, they had no equal. I cannot praise our artillery, and the men that manned those guns, enough.

As far as I'm concerned the Air Force was the most instrumental factor in winning the overall war. The armored, once free to move out, covered more area in the shortest time. But after the air corps was done, the infantry had to move in. The tanks couldn't move endlessly without infantry support. When the infantry needed something softened up or subdued in front of it, the artillery went to work.

I repeat, for the enemy, our artillery was instant hell. It also was the most effective, most destructive, most accurate, maddening, soul wrenching, ass-puckering fear instilling, fetal position generating, messengers-of-death that you and I and a whole school of artists could imagine. I say artists because to me, as a group, they appear to have the most imagination.

Back in the bocage, if an area were given a high enough priority, our artillery would put a shell in every square foot of a field. German officers upon surrendering would ask to see the "belt fed" artillery. A forward observer, usually a lieutenant carrying maps under his arm and a pair of big field glasses around his neck could, and did chase a Kraut tank using a single artillery gun. His final well-directed round of artillery landed right on top of the German tank. Further, prisoners would ask to see the "sniper scopes" on our artillery. A battery of field artillery guns was four guns—sometimes they would line up twelve guns, side by side, and fire them one after the other, one through twelve, reload and do it again. They would do this fast enough to keep a shell in the air at all times. A short point here: the Germans were told that if they surrendered, the Americans would shoot them. So many times, the prisoners would say, "Before you shoot us, can we see your such-and-such artillery?" Even when they thought they were going to die, they still wanted to see the artillery. Impressive!

Crossing the Seine

There were two outstanding times that I witnessed, when our artillery decided to knuckle down and create an Armageddon. The first time was when we had crossed a river and taken high ground in a secret and sudden, at least as far as the enemy was concerned, maneuver. After crossing the river we moved away from the river and established a line of defense. I have no idea as to how many infantrymen were involved, but would guess we made a line about two miles long and about a mile from the river. This was known as establishing a bridgehead. With a bridgehead established, the Army Corps of Engineers could then build a bridge and move a tank group across the river. Once across, the tanks could move forward to engage the enemy. This was standard practice. Foot troops across a river, build a bridge, get tanks across, and move out and ahead. For the enemy of a force on the defense, a river is an ideal place to establish a line of defense. In this particular push, we accomplished the crossing free, where "free" means "no casualties." We had not seen a single enemy. We moved in so fast that the German papers reported paratroops had been dropped in to secure the area across the river. We heard that at the time as a rumor, and I read it in our divisional book later. Once again, we knew nothing and for some reason were not dug in. We were just inside a tree line that ran to the left twenty yards, turned ninety degrees and ran for maybe eighty yards and came to a clearing. To our right front, the tree line ran about twenty yards and then turned ninety degrees to the left. Picture a stairway endwise with the flat step with a riser to the left and a riser to the right. I was in the middle of the flat step. It was about noon. We were lying there on top of the ground with our equipment off. We were on the top of the hill, flat ground immediately in front and then a deep valley. Beyond the valley, the ground rose to terminate in a wooded ridgeline. From our positions to the top of that ridge was a quarter mile by line of sight.

Well, as I said we were lying just inside the woods when some officer came running along our line. With panic in his voice and trying to hold down his volume, he kept repeating as he moved, "The Germans are attacking." "Who the hell was that?" "I don't know, I've never seen him before." Then we looked out through an opening between the brush and the trees and, lo and behold, there was what looked like the whole German Army. They were lined up between and behind tanks. How they got so close without anyone of our men seeing them I don't know. We were caught sleeping, no ifs, ands, and maybe our butts. We grabbed our gear and skedaddled-ass further into the woods. Not being dug in, we wouldn't stand a chance.

One of the guys in my squad said to another guy and me, "Hey wait, let's take a better look as to what's coming down." We stopped and went back toward our positions far enough to see them loud and clear. As we stopped, so did they. One of the tank commanders had about half his body sticking out of the turret of the tank. My buddy said, "hold it," and started putting his rifle against a tree to take good aim. Just then the turret, with its long barreled 88, started swinging and stopped right in our direction. That's enough! We made tracks to try and catch up with the rest.

The Germans had hit on a broad front, I'll guess a mile and a half to two miles wide. The units on our right were overrun. Some of the wounded were shot while lying on the ground, especially those who had some kind of a visible German souvenir on them. After traveling back a ways, we gathered and regrouped before we made it to the river. The tanks were across the river and ready to join us. An officer moved into the group that I wound up with and told us to line up between the tanks and move forward with them. At the same time going forward move right or left so as to steer yourselves to the same area you were in before retreating. The tanks did all the shooting far and near as we moved forward. When our line was reestablished, we dug in. It was reported later that there were 500 Krauts killed, wounded, and captured along the line. Maybe that line was longer than I guessed.

Right after we were back in place, we were told that the Krauts were going to attack again. For some reason I was the odd man and dug a hole by myself. It was a full depth foxhole, if I stood up and put my M1 on the parapet I could just look through the leveled sights of my rifle.

Reference note: If you throw all the ground you extract from a hole immediately around the hole, a mound or hill is formed. That mound or higher ground around the hole is called a "parapet."

Shortly after my hole was finished, the armored group assigned to our area brought up a tank with a bulldozer blade on the front. He scooped out the dirt making a trench or hole about five feet from the edge of my hole. The bulldozer backed out and away. Next, they ran a medium-sized tank into their newly dug hole. The hole was deep enough that the tank treads were completely below ground level.

Intelligence kept listening to the radio conversation going on between the German units. The word was they were going to hit us again. I don't know if it was that night or the next that the artillery was amassed behind us.

With forward observers up front, calling the shots, the artillery started its rain of death during the night. They laid down a constant barrage of shells. Some of our artillery shells contained what was known as proximity fuses. These shells explode above the ground, roughly waist high, very deadly. They were brought into use to retain this bridgehead. Every now and then, they sent flares over to light up that whole damn ridge and they just kept pouring it on. The ground rumbled to the point we could hardly sleep, and believe you me, that took some rumbling. And then, believe it or not, the Krauts came over the top and down the face of the slope the following evening. Their attack was hopeless, and suicidal.

It was still daylight when the Kraut infantry and tanks moved out and started down the open hill to our front. Our zeroed-in artillery and direct firing tanks laid into them. For them it was pure and simple suicide. Our tanks didn't use their machine guns, as the distance was too far. They used their 75 mm guns. We watched and you could actually see bodies fly in the air as the shells hit. The odd man made it to the bottom of the hill on their side. As I said, it was pure suicide on their part.

When the action started, I moved from my hole and joined a couple of guys in their hole. My thought was if the Germans give counter fire to that tank beside me I would be in a poor position if a shell ricocheted off the tank, or worse yet, if it was a high explosive shell with accompanying shrapnel.

During the night we heard two things going on. The Germans used some kind of vehicle to hook and pull their wrecked vehicles back. To us, that was weird. The other noise was their wounded crying "kommer-rod, kommer-rod." "Comrade, comrade" meant that they were surrendering and wanted us to go out and get them. Not knowing what might lie out there in the black of night, we stayed in the safety of our holes. It wasn't only this time that a German wanting to surrender yelled "comrade." It was standard procedure for them to call out like this when they wanted to give up.

After that, all was quiet on the Eastern front (their side). The following night, four Germans gave up. (They were really displaced men that the Germans had put in uniform.) They had fuses from mortar shells in their pockets. They told how they had removed them before firing them. We knew we had heard mortar shells being fired but no explosions. (When a mortar is fired it makes a very distinct sound. The sound that it made was almost identical to a single human cough. Hearing that distinctive cough sound, we always waited to hear where the mortar would hit.) One of the guys was designated to take the DP's (displaced persons) back. When they got to the aforementioned clearing behind us, they wouldn't cross it standing up for fear that one of their own would try to shoot them. They even made their guard get down to cross the field.

We didn't stay on that hill long. We moved out, flanking the front to some other area. Crossing the river and establishing a bridgehead was now accomplished.

Another thing while we were at that particular hill location, one of our pursuit planes, a P-47 Thunderbolt (15,600 of which were built during WWII) came flying low over and along the facing ridge where all the Germans were. It was low enough for us to see the pilot's face. It must have been hit, though we never saw any antiaircraft telltale black bursts. It moved along quite slowly and before going out of sight, nosed over and into the ground. It captured our complete attention because the pilot was flying so low and close. We got to see a lot of planes nose over during our tour, both Allied and enemy.

After writing the above, I went back and read the book my division put out after WWII and these are some of the facts. The river we crossed was the Seine. We were attached to Patton's Third Army at the time, and the counterattacking was occurring on a front that was two battalions wide. It all happened between August 19th and 25th. It specifically mentions my company as having been driven from the hill and Company B of the 749th tank battalion joining us to go back.

There were 30 batteries of artillery (120 guns) that were firing that night; 4,600 rounds of 105 mm and 1,048 rounds of 155 mm. According to the book, at the end of this operation, the Germans had suffered 25,000 casualties and had 12,000 prisoners taken. As to German equipment destroyed: 200 tanks, 225 artillery pieces, and 675 vehicles. Fifty German planes were shot down. These would be planes trying to destroy bridges put up by engineers, etc. They were far enough behind us that we never saw anything, and in addition, we were inside the wooded area. The crossing and beachhead was near Mantes in France and the Seine River was wide. I don't recall how my unit actually crossed it, more than likely boats of some kind.

Crossing the Rhine

The second time we witnessed a real artillery output was crossing the Rhine River. The artillery was softening up the defenses
on the far side of the Rhine. The actual figures, once again,
come from my divisional book: 1,250 artillery pieces of varying
size fired 300,000 rounds of ammunition in one hour. It was the
greatest bombardment of all time, period. It was like the Fourth
of July finale that continued for an hour. Each gun fired a round
every 15 seconds, continuously for an hour. Calculating each gun
to be 10 feet wide (the bipods for stabilization extended sideways
at an angle) and putting them side-by-side, there would be a line
of artillery guns, 2.2 miles long. Quite a firing line! Eisenhower,
along with the commanding generals of the Ninth Army and
XVI Corps, visited the night the record-making "boom-boom"
boys did their softening up work. The 79th was part of the XVI
Corps, not that that meant a big rat's butt.

My regiment was in reserve and crossed just before mid-morning. The other two regiments did the initial crossing, starting in
the dark, while the big bombardment was still going on. For all
practical purposes, there was next to no resistance.

One of the things I recall was that after we were on the far side
and moving inland and parallel to the Rhine, the Germans sent
some pursuit planes in to strafe and bomb the bridges that were
going up. Our ack-ack (antiaircraft) guns had moved up to their
defensive positions. The ack-ack put up a black puff wall that
you would think nothing could get through. Not so. Those damn
planes flew right through it. We were under the fringe of that
black umbrella as we walked. Every now and then as we walked
along, we could hear a piece of shrapnel hit the ground. As far
as I know, the ack-ack never hit any of us either. The Rhine River
crossing was toward the end of March 1945.

MORE ARTILLERY STUFF

Fire for Effect

Let's add a little definition to the artillery. Like I said, a battery was four artillery pieces and a lot of times our side used 3 batteries together for 12 guns in all. The gunners and ammunition personnel were not out of harm's way. There was a lot of counter firing going on between their artillery and ours. Enemy artillery was considered a prime target. A Piper Cub in the air spotting their artillery, directing counter fire on it, and knocking it out helped the infantry tremendously.

Our artillery was great, but it did have a negative side. Every now and then they would fire a "short" round. That short round could, and sometimes did, come in on us. We would turn the air blue with appropriate words and settle back down. One day we were on the move and walking along a wooded area. An asshole spotter in a Piper plane thought we were Krauts and called for fire on us. The first salvo, probably 12 shells, was right on target, killing 3. Radio contact established who we were, and "what an asshole" moved off.

The best artillery unit that we enjoyed having behind and with us was the 999th Field Artillery Battalion. They were all black (Afro-American) and they were good. When we saw an Afro-American officer up with or moving around us, we knew the 999th was behind. They were forward observers for the artillery and always wore a big set of field glasses and carried a folded map, open or in a case. Afro-Americans were not assigned to the infantry in WWII, so their forward observers were always easy to spot. The 999th never dropped a short round.

One of our guys was back one time and watched the 999th guys in action. The fire commander would yell the numbers for the artillery piece's vertical and horizontal settings, then yell, "Hitler, count yo' children ... fire!" They used a rhythm for loading and firing their guns and they made their guns dance while pushing those blind merciless shells into the air. Once again, a shell in the air at all times. We admired and respected the 999th.

Another picturesque story: we were dug in, in a wooded area. Forward and out on a corner of the wooded area, we had a two-man observation post, which was a well camouflaged hole that had a phone in it. The observers in the hole were there to do just that: keep an eye out and report, by way of the telephone, anything that they might see that is going on to the front. The ground ahead was flat for three hundred yards, and then there was a railroad track that ran from right to left. The train tracks were on a three to four foot high dirt embankment. I went up, sent or otherwise, to check the outpost. The guys told me the Krauts were on the other side of the tracks straight ahead. After watching for a little, sure enough, one stood up and moved. I got on the phone and asked to be connected with the artillery. Artillery control asked me if I could direct fire. I told them I never had but sure would try. They told me to hang on and they would get back with me. I can't recall how long we watched and waited, but eventually an officer came sliding into the hole with us. We showed him where they were hanging around and then someone on their side obligingly moved. He referred to his map and asked for a single round. It hit way left and behind. He gave them corrected coordinates and said, "Fire for effect." I knew he had 3 batteries working with him. Let me add here, some field artillery guns fire low trajectory and some fire with a high arch. The ones behind us were low trajectory. When those shells came over us, the other two guys went down instinctively, as the noise of the shells skimming the treetops came through loud and clear. I told myself this guy is a pro and if he is next to me, I should be OK. I resisted the impulse to go down and watched the shells land. They all hit on top of the tracks and smack dab on target. I asked the officer, "What happened? You said fire for effect but I only saw four shells hit." His answer was, "No you didn't, you saw twelve shells hit." So there! Impressive again!

Night Time

When I started to tell about the 88s and our fear of them, we were back in the hedgerows in late June and July. Crossing the Rhine occurred in late March, or nine months later. We, you the reader and I, covered a lot of territory fast to get to the artillery stories. Let's move back to the bocage, "maudit" or otherwise.

In the hedgerows, if there were a large field ahead of us, and we stopped for the night, listening posts were set up. The listeners would move out in front of the rest and stand, or I should say sit, and just look around and listen. You have never done it, I'm sure, so I'll tell you. At night, when you sit and look or stare at something for a prolonged period, your imagination plays hell with you and you start seeing things. The things you "see" are your imagined fears. You have to look away and then back to confirm your doubts. If your buddy is right beside you, you can whisper and get confirmation. Most of the time, we had a guy on top of the hedgerow and another at the base.

If the moon was half out, it was worse than full dark or bright moonlight. We were all warned about seeing things in the dark, and yet we still did. As an example, you would look at the corner of a three-pole break in the hedgerow and think that if a Kraut were trying to get close, he would crawl under the lowest pole. Stare at it a while and something would start taking shape. You really get on edge with your doubts. "If I fire at it, will those yahoos on line fire blindly while I or we are here? Do I fire at nothing and get laughed at or catch hell? Will I give away our position? What are you going to do? What are you going to dooo?" Listening posts were not the way to keep your natural hair color, and if you had any faith in God before, it increased as you talked and made promises to Him.

Speaking of giving your position away, there was a plane the Germans sent over most nights for reconnaissance. He flew over and took pictures. His motor had a very distinct on-and-off purr to it. He was called "Bed Check Charlie." We were told not to fire at him even if you could see him, the idea being he couldn't tell where our lines or any other personnel were. He came so many times we mentally made notes to expect him. The Air Force added a P-38 M twin fuselage night fighter to its array of weapons. The plane was equipped with radar or night vision. They put a few Bed Check Charlies to bed permanently and after that, Bed Check Charlie or his replacement was rarely seen.

FIRST DEAD

The first real impression I got from looking at our own dead American soldiers was not long after joining my outfit in the bocage. I had seen an odd one here and there but this was different. For some reason, I was alone and as I walked past this big barn-like structure, I glanced in the open door. I could see what looked like a couple of guys lying there. My curiosity being piqued, I hesitated then turned into the doorway for a better look. The whole floor was covered with dead GIs, all on their backs and laid straight out. The graves detail must have used that place for a temporary site or morgue. I didn't need or want vivid pictures like that, so ... look away and keep moving.

FIRST REAL ACTION

The very first action I was involved in was in the hedgerows, not many days after being assigned to the 79th. It couldn't have been too many days after, as we still had our bayonets. We were moving along slowly toward an opening into a field and not too far before the opening stood our company commander. He was speaking in a hushed tone and saying, "Fix bayonets; they are right in that field." He repeated the same thing to about every third guy. Before I was fully through the opening, those ahead of me had started firing. A few seconds later I saw a German moving forward and to the top of the hedgerow at the far end of the field. He saw us and was gone in a flash. He came and went before anyone could fire even if they tried to shoot from the hip. There were two large bomb craters in the field and two Germans were in one. When the firing stopped, the two in the crater were wounded and there was a third, now dead, lying along the left edge of the field. They couldn't have been on guard, otherwise they would have started firing at us before we moved into the same field with them.

To give you an idea of how little hatred I had for the Germans, I bandaged up one of them. He was old, at least in my eyes, and I took pity on him. He looked at me with wonder as I bandaged him and he had the typical look of someone in shock.

We wound up digging in, in that same field, and after spreading out evenly, hole to hole, my buddy and I dug in about five feet from the dead German. The weather was warm and the next morning, while my buddy and I were still in our hole, a few guys started arguing about getting rid of that corpse. Three of them were trying to argue the rest into giving them a hand to move the body. I grew impatient fast and climbing out of my hole I grabbed one of the arms of the body and said, "Where to?" We moved said German into one of the bomb craters and using the loose dirt covered him. No services were held but we did stick his rifle in the ground and we placed or hung his helmet on top.

Incidentally, we came across a lot of German rifles in our meanderings. Some were rifles from prisoners or just lying there for whatever reason. We never liked to leave a working piece of enemy equipment lying around so we usually took the rifles by the barrel and whacked it against a tree or anything else that was sturdy enough to break the stock off. Their standard rifle was a single shot, magazine-loaded, bolt-action piece, and the wooden stock, though shaped and sanded out, had no finish of any kind on it. They must have thought that it was a waste of time to put a finish on the wood back at the place they were manufactured. They were definitely not as good as our M1s, but they were just as accurate. If we came across any other German weapon that we thought might be serviceable, we tried to render it useless. If it was an artillery piece we closed its breach and put a grenade down the muzzle. Grenades were useful and had more functions than just antipersonnel weapons.

ORIGIN OF NAME

Before I forget, I'd like to let you know how the division got its name and divisional patch insignia. In WWI, late in 1918, a suggestion was put out: Why don't the different units suggest a name and design for a patch, to be worn on the left arm of their uniforms? The 79th had distinguished itself in the Lorraine sector of France. The white "Croix de Lorraine" on a blue background was a symbol of triumph, dating back nearly 500 years and was well known, hence the adoption of it for a patch.

The Free French Interior (FFI) or the French Underground used the same symbol during WWII. Whenever the FFI were around or caused a "happening," they would scratch the Lorraine cross on a wall, building, etc., to let the "Bosch" know they had been there. We came across their scratches a lot. The FFI were merciless and the Germans feared and hated them. The German retribution on a village where an underground act was committed was, at times, worse than merciless. They might kill one, ten, or the whole village in retribution or in search of names of the FFI underground. Hatred went both ways. I won't dwell on this subject anymore, other than to add that later on, a high-ranking German officer listed one of the conditions of his surrendering, including himself and a couple hundred men and all their equipment, was that neither he nor any of his men would be turned over to the FFI.

BACK TO THE BOCAGE AGAIN

Since the walls of dirt, rocks, brush, and trees were so easily defended, it appeared that the fighting would be endless. Then some sergeant, in maintenance I think, came up with the idea to build a pointed plow, built like the snowplows used to clear roads in the northern U.S., with a V-shaped frame, but without the sheet metal covering the surface of the plow. The frame was made from railroad tracks, which were taken from the beachhead area in Normandy, where they had previously served as antitank obstacles. There were plenty of these obstacles around, free for the taking. (As the British would say, "A plentiful supply, really!") The frame was mounted on the front of a 35 ton medium-sized tank, and it wasn't long before new openings were being made in the hedgerows, each one with a tank coming through it, and the hedgerows were no longer a major obstacle. This was Yankee ingenuity at work and BREAKTHROUGH! As a point of clarification, one tank or even a few tanks would not venture into a covered area without infantry support, but when they traveled in a mass formation, they moved forward, with or without the infantry.

Joe Lopez

JOE LOPEZ

When I first joined the Cross of Lorraine, my assistant squad leader was Joe Lopez and the squad leader was Elmo Lobstein. It's Joe that I would like to tell you about, and I think Joe deserves a whole chapter. ...So to Joe.

Now this guy was a character. Of all the guys who came and went and whom I got to know and serve Army time with, in or out of combat, Joe impressed me the most.

Joe was a married man, around three or four years older than I, had an average to slim build, and was about five ten or eleven. He was of Mexican descent, fine-featured and probably born in California, which was his home state. He spoke Spanish, and with that he could get by talking to the French. When it came to begging for food in French, he was totally literate.

Patrols

A Mexican is supposed to be a combination of Spanish and American Indian. The Spanish showed in his sharp or fine nose and the Indian showed in his ability to move through leaves, twigs, and brush, not unlike a cat. In Army boots like the rest of us, not moccasins, he seemed to instinctively move quietly. I like to think he was as quiet as a shy mouse, running across a hardwood floor in a convent. I used to watch him purposely. Where others picked their feet up and down as they walked, Joe's feet glided and skimmed the ground. Overall, Joe was a natural leader but it took me a while to realize it.

When it came to patrols, reconnaissance mostly, Joe's abilities became known early on. His name spread until it was known throughout the battalion. If they needed a special patrol made up of the pick of the battalion, Joe would be one of the members. An officer normally led a battalion patrol. If it were a company or platoon patrol, Joe would be in charge, and he never appointed others to go with him—you had to volunteer.

One patrol I went on with him is worth sharing, as I thought I made an ass of myself at the time, and it was funny. (It's good to be able to laugh at one's self, sometimes.) We were supposed to move out of this town we were temporarily stopped in, and reconnoiter the area to the front to see if there were any Jerries about. There were five of us and after we had covered about a quarter mile, we came across a stream, too wide to jump, and about knee deep. The first two guys waded across and as I watched, I came up with an inspirational idea. Rifle slung across my shoulder, I shinnied up a tree with the intention of having the bent tree deposit me on the far dry bank. Unfortunately, the diameter of the tree was not proper for the load: the tree bent too early and deposited me in the middle of the creek. We had a laugh and I, too, had to change my socks later. We went ahead, with squishing feet, as far as Joe led us, but saw nothing.

When we got back to town (wading the creek again, of course), to our surprise, our unit was gone. This is where we changed socks. Our spare socks were carried, unfolded, inside our shirts, dry, and non-cumbersome. Taking off after our unit, we caught up with them where they were strung out along a blacktop road that led out of a town to our right. The Jerries were in the town and didn't know we were anywhere around. The road made a curve to our right and on into the village.

The first thing we knew, a Kraut jeep came around the curve heading toward us. The driver and two passengers saw us, but too late. They stepped on the gas and tried to run the gauntlet, made up of M1s and two machine guns. Their souls were promptly dispatched.

The next thing that came around the corner was a Jerry truck with Red Cross banners on it. We tried to wave it down but force was required. The driver elected to have his soul follow the two soldiers in the German jeep. His cargo was arms and ammo, rather than medical.

And now some clanking noise, and around the curve, but off the road, came a tank. Now it was our turn to skedaddle, across an opening and into the woods. We didn't sing "Through the woods, to grandmother's house we go," but rather, "Make room, I'm coming through." Like I said, you don't stand a chance with a tank when you're in the open.

A little while later our people moved a tank destroyer up and into place. Now it was the German tank's turn to use his reverse gear, and he did, right on out of sight.

A totally armored vehicle without machine guns, armor on front, a Two more points of interest: After dark that night, I was moving around for whatever reason and I unknowingly stepped on a guy in his hole. Pulling the tree stunt and stepping into the other guy's hole in the same day was giving my batting average a bad turn.

The second amusing point was that our people laid mines on the road, after dark. This was to hold the night traffic down. Later on, we heard the distinctive clip-clop, clip-clop of a horse on the blacktop. We said, "This is going to be something else." Our only option was to sit and wait for the inevitable, and maybe imagine what the inevitable was going to look like. (We were dug in along the woods, not on the road.) Now who'd a thunk it? That horse went the full length and beyond and never touched a mine. All those that had watched it were happy the horse had won. If we had been somewhere else, other than on line, I'm sure that horse would have received a standing ovation. (Do you think angels watch over horses?)

One time back in the hedgerows, Joe slid into the hole that another guy and I had buddied up on. Joe's first words were, "I think I'm going to puke." We said, "Why? And make sure it's outside of our hole." Lopez filled us in about the patrol he had just returned from. It was a reconnaissance patrol and one of the guys had made the mistake (how was anyone to know, really?) of looking over the top of the hedgerow in the wrong place. It must have been that the Kraut had that particular spot zeroed in or our man looked too long. The slug hit him right in the forehead. Joe being right next to him saw him face up as he fell to the ground. The price of war!

When we were told to move forward and go into the attack, we knew the Germans were somewhere near and to our front. We could expect to make contact anywhere from a quarter mile up. Or maybe not at all, as they sometimes moved out just ahead of us. Anyway, as we first started moving, Joe would have to do a number 2. His bowels worked that way, nerves probably. He always caught right up. Most of the rest of us had the reaction of being nauseated and not wanting to eat until the situation was resolved. After the war, I asked an MD about that. He said he thought it was because the body goes into "alert" mode. When you eat, the priority for the blood becomes the stomach. The "alert" mode sends the blood to the brain and tries to empty the stomach so no blood is required. Sounds reasonable.

In our migration across France, Joe always seemed to keep track of the houses in the area. When we stopped and were told to dig in, he always knew of that house we had or hadn't passed. If there were none to the rear he would reconnoiter to the front. All of us would start digging and if you looked around, Joe would be gone. His mission was to find food. Like I said, his Spanish covered all the ingredients of a French menu. Since we were usually the first Americans the French saw, the farmhouses were always kind to their liberators. His normal fare was eggs, bread, and butter and sometimes "confiture." [Confiture: French for "jam" or "preserves."] Joe didn't go out scrounging for food every day, but enough to make us jealous. When he came back he would move in with a couple others whose hole was big enough.

When it came to begging coffee off of any of us, Joe had no equal. He would move into a group that was sipping their coffee, and would say, "Is your coffee hot? Is it sweet? Let me taste it," and keep begging. Invariably, he got his sips. Don't get me wrong, Joe was respected by all. Most enjoyed his light banter and would smile at his playful begging.

Joe had two pet phrases that he kept repeating. "I keep telling those Germans, don't f*** with the U.S." and "I keep telling those bastards, you have to get up early if you are going to try and get ahead of the U. S. of A."

As I said, Joe was an assistant squad leader when I joined, then promoted to squad leader and then on up to platoon guide. The last move made him right hand man to the lieutenant who was the platoon leader. Being promoted and next to the brass, Joe's foraging and begging had to be surrendered in favor of a more serious life.

He got wounded two or three times and I don't remember the last time. I know I was there a couple of times when he came back. He had made comments to me about my being there for his return. It was always hard for anyone to come "back," after having tasted the quiet and safety of the rear. When you did get back, it was nice to see a face you knew, and more so a friend. I know Joe wasn't there at the war's end, but he was there when we crossed the Rhine River, and he did make it home because he wrote to me after we were both home.

Joe and the Silver Star

The story of how Joe Lopez was awarded the Silver Star is amusing and entertaining, I hope. The award was for meritorious action above and beyond the call of duty. Right on, Joe!

As I said before, it's good to begin at the start. You have to get a picture of pre-combat Joe vs. combat Joe. He told me this story and I think I remember it well.

Back in England, Company I personnel had been acting up while on pass and—of course—frequenting the local pubs. The captain called the company together and warned them that the next bad report that he received, he would ground the company, and no one would be getting a pass to town. Later the following week, the captain mustered the company and said he would like them to know that they were all grounded, and why. He then called upon Joe to do a front and center and to read a letter, out loud, to all.

The letter explained how this particular soldier, who was inebriated beyond good sense and comportment, was acting unruly. The town constables gave him a choice of getting himself under control or returning to his camp, at which point, one Joe Lopez unbuttoned his fly and began to relieve himself in the street. After Joe read the letter's respectful closing, the captain took over. He allowed the snickering to die down and after a prolonged silence said, "Now you know! ... Joe Lopez, you can return to your place."

The scene now switches to France and we find that captain lying wounded in the middle of a field. He cannot move under his own power. The field is covered by at least one enemy machine gun. The captain yells orders to the rest to leave him alone or "they'll get you, too." Just as the sun starts to set, the captain hears something. Turning, he sees a low-crawling body coming to him. Trying not to make any noise, the captain remained quiet. When the two of them were safe, the captain did speak, and I quote Joe, who was quoting the captain, "Of all the sons of bitches to come out there after me, it had to be you, Lopez." Wear that Silver Star proud, Joe!

I always had confidence in Joe. Without exaggeration, I can say I would follow him anywhere. As I mentioned previously, I was there to welcome him back each time and I think he got to respect my seniority or, more accurately, my luck.

Shoe on the Other Foot

There was another story about Joe that I recall with amusement. It was mid-September '44, and Joe had been hit once and returned. We were trucked up to a certain point, then told to unload and form a line of skirmishes. My thought at the time was, we are going into the attack and we've got the trucks with us, what the hell is coming down? Did someone back there get the idea that we can attack by the truckload? But it wasn't long before the trucks were gone.

We moved forward maybe a quarter of a mile and we came to the base of a high hill. We were actually on the west face of it. The hill had the same barren slope, going to our right, as far as we could see. To our left, maybe 50 yards, the hill turned so that its slope faced the north. The city of Charmes was at the base of the north slope. Beyond the city, to the east, was the Moselle River. My platoon's job was to go up the hill and take the high ground south of Charmes. We advanced halfway up the hill when a German machine gun, to our immediate front, let loose.

His first burst did not clear the crest of the hill and kicked up the ground. All of us were now flat on the slope and looking up. The lieutenant called back and a mortar unit in support quickly dispatched the Kraut machine gunner.

We no sooner started to move when a machine gun to our far right made it sound like bees going by. Our defense was to lie as flat as possible and hope. That Kraut kept on us. He was really in front of our right flanking element and we had to wait until they quieted him. It took a bit so we had a chance to relax into the ground. I happened to be near the lieutenant when he received word "all-clear." I got up and looking over, saw Lopez lying flat in a gully or wash. The gully was made from the rain running off the top of the hill. It was a good defensive spot as Joe was nearly below ground level. He had his face turned away from me. I stood right over him and said with a fatherly tone, "OK, Joe, you can get up now." He turned to me and said, "McDonnell, you son of a bitch, you." For a switch, the shoe was on the other foot and I loved the moment as I lorded it over Joe.

> *Postscript: After writing the above, I learned that Joe died a few years back. In combat, he did his job well and he was a natural leader and I take comfort in knowing that he was not left lying white-faced, open-eyed, rigid, and cold in some unknown field in France. May his soul rest in peace. (Do you think a person has to bum coffee in heaven, sometimes? ... Naaaah!)*

NOW, FOR THE TOP OF THE HILL

With the machine gunner on our extreme right quieted down, and with Joe Lopez up (oh, how I wish he could read this!), we resumed the advance to the top of the hill, where we came across and into a wooded area. When you move through woods, it's important to keep contact with those on both sides. If one unit advances beyond another and you run into trouble, one unit can be firing on another, unknowingly. As we advanced, we were a little disorganized in that we had migrated into groups rather than a straight continuous line. All at once the guys on our left came running to us and said they heard Germans talking to our left. We yelled to our right, "Get the rest of the platoon." Like in the movies: "Call for some back up." Well, we made so much noise yelling the Germans thought we were a whole company. The Germans were expecting an attack from the north and were facing north. We were behind them so we caught them by total surprise. They moved out and ran down the hill in front of them, which put them out of the woods and into the clear, mostly. We moved farther forward and into a clearing. We started shooting, adding additional motivation to their run. I'm sure you remember running down a hill as a kid. The trick is to keep your legs under you. It was amusing, really. They made unsteady targets.

In front of us in a clearing was some kind of structure with a low obelisk, maybe 30 feet high, and a concrete railing with some heavy-duty large diameter support pillars. The railing must have been 18 inches wide and a minimum of four inches thick. Our guys ran over behind the railing, and with something to support their guns took better pot shots. It wasn't long before the Germans were out of sight.

The next thing that happened was that some Krauts started to return fire with a machine gun. They were a little beyond the base of the hill and in one of the houses that bordered the city. Their machine gun started chipping away at the posts, railing, and the concrete obelisk. We could see which house the gunner was firing from. It was on the edge of town. We figured we would keep him busy until we could get a mortar on him. Some guys took a helmet, on the end of a stick, and raised it above the railing level, and the machine gunner blasted away—right out of an old movie.

Soon we could see some of our guys moving through the streets of the town. We kept that German machine gun busy until our guys went in the back of the machine gunner's house. After that, we got up and walked around.

Lo and behold, that obelisk had our divisional insignia on it. We figured that our division had taken that hill in WWI. We felt a sense of awe and pride. In fact, the monument had been erected in honor of the French forces for stopping the Germans' WWI westward drive at the Moselle River. All French forces take pride in the Cross of Lorraine. For them, it is almost like their national flag.

Between the obelisk and the railing was, and still is, a table. On the table is a map cast in stone and covered with something like clear, transparent stone. It identifies all the different French Army units, by name and number, which were amassed there in WWI, and in color yet. It's beautiful! My wife Marguerite and I have visited there twice in recent years. The second time was with Mike Cousin and his wife Monica. The chippings on the posts by the German machine gun are still visible and I got a kick out of examining them as they made my memories real. The concrete obelisk has been covered by a steel sheet metal covering, and the plain metal surface no longer has a Cross of Lorraine on its face side, or the side that faces the city, but now has the Cross of Lorraine on the reverse side.

One other thing before we leave the hill: Two or three hours after all was quiet, one of the guys found a German weapon. No one had seen one like it. It was a form of grenade launcher assembly that mounted on the standard German .30 caliber bolt-action rifle. In essence, it did the same as our grenade launcher that I mentioned earlier. The difference was that theirs had a device on the side with distance graduation on it, and a level indicator. I think the idea was that you estimated the distance to the target, set the distance on the graduated device and then leveled the level indicator. The first round fired might not be right, but the readjustment would make you much more accurate when firing the next round. There was also some ammunition for it.

The lieutenant said, "Before we send it back to ordinance, let's give it a try. Make your best guess and see how close you can come to that clump of bushes on the right, down there." Someone did as he said and came quite close. Three or four Germans came out of the clump and ran like rabbits. No one had a chance to shoot them before they were out of sight behind bigger bushes.

Militarily, our strategy was to take the town, cross the river, and establish controlled ground on the Germans' side. The Germans blew up the only bridge going from the town across the Moselle, and they blew it almost right in the face of our troops. The four

Germans that were flushed from the clump of bushes must have swum across the river, if they crossed it at all.

We remained on that hill several days at least. On the last day there, Bing Crosby and Dinah Shore came to the city of Charmes to put on a USO show. They were not only within artillery range but almost rifle range of the enemy. There were two shows scheduled. The one in the afternoon went on according to schedule, but just as the evening show was about to start, word came to the 79th, "Saddle up, we're moving out." The evening show was cancelled for lack of audience. Later, we did cross the Moselle River, but not right there at the city of Charmes.

MEDALS

Motivations

It is with mixed emotions that I add this part about medals, but I said earlier that I would, so I will. There were some who received medals that truly deserved them, while others didn't. Most actions taken in combat were for one or more of the following reasons: 1) to perform your assigned task of taking the assigned ground and/or objective; 2) to kill the enemy if they did not retreat or surrender; 3) to protect your unit or group; 4) to protect yourself. Without the group, no one can survive for long. To preserve yourself, you preserve others. In preserving yourself, you preserved others.

When you asked someone why he did what he did, the usual answer was "I don't know, I just acted." In the interest of putting definition to that non-premeditated action, I think it was to preserve their buddies and themselves. It is or was their way of solving the immediate problem at hand, as they saw it, and/or the means of doing the job that needed to be done. I'm sure some have had a guilt feeling about something they thought they could have done or should have done better, after a given action. Maybe that in turn motivated them to try harder the next time. Soldiers faced with terror and death, for the first time in their lives or the tenth time for that matter, might choke up and freeze. They never tell anyone, because they perceive themselves as having done something wrong or cowardly, when in reality, their actions were normal. Are they awarded medals for carrying on, even under that oh-so-normal feeling of guilt? Understand this: I am not talking about any one in particular, and certainly not myself, but most dogfaces, or any one else that really faced dying in combat. If I were to try to pick a prime example of whom this happened to, I would pick the troops that went in on the initial invasion, as they were new and inexperienced. The next group I would pick would be the new replacements in combat.

When all hell breaks loose and you are there in the open, your body tenses up as tight as it can in anticipation of being hit and the mind starts racing with the questions "what do I do?" or "what can I do?" The more inexperienced you are in combat, the more you have a tendency to freeze. It is extremely hard to get up and move, especially when all the others around you are lying flat. What to do? What to do? The Army manual had an all-encompassing phrase, "It depends on the situation and the terrain." When you get right down to it, the phrase is correct. Should I move to the right or left, forward or back, or should I lie here and pretend that I am dead? Maybe I can make a quick jump and land behind that guy over there and then I will at least have something between the enemy and me. Part of the answers: If it is artillery fire (only) coming in, and you have nothing that will protect you, you have got to MOVE. If it is a tank and you don't have real good cover, you have got to MOVE. If you are under machine gun and enemy rifle fire and it is close in, now is the time to consider moving right, left, forward, or back. To check the terrain you move your head slowly (slower than that) and try to pick out something or anything that you can get behind, or between you and the enemy, as you make your move. In looking for a path that takes you to the enemy, you have to turn your face to him and more fear sets in as your thoughts tell you that the enemy is on the other end of that rifle and he is watching YOU, and you know the enemy will react to anything he sees that is moving. These judgements as to what action to take have to be learned in combat and as hard as it is, you have to make the choice based on what you think is the best move for you and your group.

You might have experienced a bad dream, a nightmare, in which you could not move, walk, or run because your fear was too strong. You might have woken up with your heart racing loudly, and possibly you were really sweating. That semiconscious fear would simulate being in combat, but then you wake up, and as the fear subsides, you breathe a sigh of relief and say, "Thank God it was only a dream." So like I said, when all hell breaks loose, and the dogface hits the ground, his nightmare has started and when he opens his eyes he consciously keeps living it. Does he deserve a medal for controlling and overcoming his fears enough to allow him to move and do what he thinks is right? So many of us thought that, regarding medals, the greatest heroes by far, were the ones that "bought it" or died. Their medal was the Purple Heart ...posthumously.

I don't want to sound like sour grapes, but just after the war had ended, the captain of our company told us he had a number of medals that had been allotted to our company, and if we wanted one, we should write out our own recommendation. To the best of my knowledge, no one did. Even Lopez used to tell me that he knew his Silver Star would not buy him a cup of coffee when he returned home. A purple heart was awarded to every man wounded in combat, one for each separate time wounded. Fine! In summary there were a hell of a lot who deserved being recognized with a medal, and at the same time there was a flip side as to how and to whom they were doled out.

Medics

There was one valiant group that never seemed to receive the recognition and honors they were so entitled to. They were the on line medics, one to each platoon. That meant one medic for each thirty men, and that's not bad. They carried no weapons and their only defense was the Red Cross symbol on their helmet and an armband with the same. The Red Cross with its white background was the symbol of neutrality, but the incoming artillery and mortar shells did not recognize it. The medics' "job" was to administer first aid and try to do all possible to keep the wounded alive long enough for them to be picked up and taken to the battalion aid station. We could be pinned down with our bellies closer to the ground than a pancake on a greaseless skillet and someone would yell, "MEDIC!" Damn if they didn't come, bent over, on the run and fully exposed. Talk about dedication! They were truly the unsung heroes of combat. I have never seen estimates of the number of lives they saved. Their equipment was one or two bags with long shoulder straps. These were very handy to go on or off the shoulder as needed. Picture a medic running to a downed and wounded dogface, going down on one knee next to the wounded and at the same time pulling his first aid bag off his shoulder, or pulling the bag to his front while the strap remained on his shoulder, opening the bag and doing it all automatically. This is what I mean when I say the design of the bag made it handy. The bags contained various bandages, medical tape, morphine injection capsules, tourniquets, sulfa powder to sprinkle on wounds, and different pairs of scissors. The on line medics were brave, brave men indeed!

ANOTHER CROSSING

I don't remember the place we moved to after Charmes, but the next major event in my memory was crossing the Meurthe River. My company was in support, as another group had crossed ahead of us. Once again, you didn't know squat, until squat hit you in the face.

We came to a narrow river with a makeshift bridge across it. The bridge was made of pontoon boats, side by side, with loose wooden planks lying across the boats. Two planks wide was sufficient for infantry to file across. We could hear small arms fire to the front, and around. I remember, too, that there was a war correspondent there. What made him stand out was that he had neither gear nor weapon. His left shoulder had a patch of some kind and at the top it said "correspondent."

As we walked across the bridge, a dog ran across, heading in the same direction. On the far side were bushes about five or six feet high. Beyond the bushes was a clearing, maybe two hundred yards deep, and beyond that was an elevated blacktop road.

The unit that had preceded us, probably before daylight, was dug in or digging in along the road. The Germans must have spotted us because they laid in machine gun fire, big time.

Lying flat, we kept backing down the bank of the river until our feet were in the water. All at once, we heard a loud yelp. We said, "Uh oh, that dog got hit," then, "Medic!"

We saw the medic move to the left front of where we were lying. Bullets had stopped flying so we moved to where the medic was. He was feeling and examining the prostrate yelper. It wasn't the dog; it was one of our guys. Then the medic said, "He's OK, he just fainted."

Someone picked up the guy's helmet and upon examining it could see where a bullet had gone in the front and followed the inside curvature between the steel helmet and the helmet liner. The bullet came out the back and had not touched his head. He had yelped and passed out. Never did find out where that dog wound up.

We moved as best we could to the left and then forward until we were on the left flank of that dug-in bunch along the road. We crossed the road and got into some woods. Then all hell broke loose again. The first shells that came in on us burst aerially in the trees. They killed our company first sergeant, who happened to be with my platoon. He was an old-timer with the platoon, but young in years. There were a couple others wounded, too. On the second firing, I got hit. I was flat on my belly and it hit me in the back, just above the belt. It was hotter than hell and then it seemed it was burning on my stomach side. Had it gone through me and was I feeling blood coming out of my stomach? In any case, I wasn't in any position to do a physical inspection. I got up and moved maybe twenty feet, paralleling the road. My thoughts were moving fast as I figured they had us zeroed in and could see us. As I moved, the lieutenant said, "Across the road," and I said, "No, go along the road." We started to move and the lieu-tenant and I were no more than fifteen feet apart when a shell hit right in between us. We were both knocked down, and both of us were dazed. We got up, looked at each other, and never said a word. Directly between him and me was a missing patch of sod, about 18 to 24 inches in diameter, and the ground was smoking. We moved back a bit into the woods and nothing more came in on us. There was a clearing between the Jerries and us, running from left to right with railroad tracks running through the middle of it. Beyond the tracks were more woods. We were supposed to move into the woods as far as we could.

The first or second guy across the tracks had an antitank gun fire at him. From that point on, the rest of us wasted no time when it was our turn to cross the tracks. I mentioned my buddy Kraff earlier. As he jumped the tracks, he held his rifle high and with both arms extended. That Jerry antitank gunner's timing was good, but not good enough. The shell passed right in front of his belt. We moved into the woods and we knew the Krauts were there too. They had a tank in there that was making a hell of a lot of noise. We dug in.

Later, after dark, I was sent back along with a detail of four or five others for the next day's rations. We had to go back to where we had crossed the river. After picking up the boxes of K-rations and 5 gallon jerrycans of water, we headed back. (I don't know why the Army called them jerrycans.)

The route we picked to return to our dug-in squad first followed a straight line from the river to the road. Along the near side of the road were GIs that had preceded us in the initial attack, who had also dug in for the night. Our route then turned left at the road and followed it until reaching our own area. It was pitch dark out, except on the road where a German vehicle still burned. Well, the Germans spotted us moving via the light from the burning vehicle.

141

Just as we got to the road, Jerry put a couple rounds of artillery on us. The shells were low trajectory and seemed to cross the road and hit right behind us. I dove into what I saw was the outline of a hole with a guy in it. It seems his buddy was outside of the hole and although he jumped in his hole, I beat him to it and he wound up on top of me. The poor guy got hit. I got out of the hole, picked up my box of K's and kept going.

I never reported the back wound. I have a scar and had it x-rayed after I returned from service, but they found nothing. Maybe the scar was only from the burn. No report, no purple heart. Life's a bitch, eh?

After the Meurthe River fun, the objective became the Forest of Parroy (Foret de Parroy). Let me repeat simply and to the point, fighting to take ground in the forest is hell, hell, and more hell. One of the big negatives is artillery bursts in the trees. When you sit still, you have to dig in and you always have to put a cover on your hole. Dig the hole first. Cover most of the hole with branches, allowing yourself room to get in and out. Then pile loose dirt on top of the branches, to a depth of at least six inches. Six inches was usually enough to stop the shrapnel from an aerial or tree burst.

When you exited your hole and moved out and forward, forget protection. You never knew what you would run into: snipers, camouflaged infantry, hidden tanks, field pieces, mines, or what. Some areas were very dense, and the complete lack of sunshine would become demoralizing. What a trip!

I think it was this Forest of Parroy that Hitler had fought in during WWI, and it held special memories for him. His orders were to "hold, at all costs." That S.O.B. had memories of a place he had been to, so now his soldiers and our soldiers would go through hell, suffer, and die just because he had fought there. I wonder how many lives that cost?

HOLES FOR THE LIVING

I just mentioned how we dug in the woods. Let me expand a little here about hole digging. We just about always dug a hole for the night, and most of the time we paired off to dig. Sometimes, if there was an odd man, he would dig in with two others or dig in by himself. There were some exceptions to digging in, just as there are to most rules.

After dark, and in a wooded area where you might hit tree roots or if the soil was rocky, we would dig a slit trench. A slit trench was a shallow hole that was just deep enough so that a man lying on his side would be below ground level. Usually, you tried to dig it wide enough to at least have room enough to manage turning from one side to the other, one guy at a time of course.

When digging in after dark, doing it quietly was an important factor. When you were digging in rocky soil, you broadcasted to all where you were. Can you imagine a steel shovel striking rock in an atmosphere of dead silence? Now have 40 to 50 holes being dug at the same time. Hitting and digging tree roots in the dark was also fun. You felt its shape and direction by hand and then tried to cut it with your entrenching tool. The shape of the blade of entrenching tool was about 8 to 9 inches wide and 12 inches long, V-shaped on the cutting end and made of steel. The wooden handle was about 15 inches long. The steel blade could be straight out from the handle, folded against the handle or turned and locked ninety degrees to the handle, for chopping. It was a very well designed, effective tool. If the ground was good for digging, we would go to "kneel up height" for depth. If we knew we would be staying longer than a day or were told we were going to be counterattacked, we went full depth. After our rifle, our entrenching tool was the most important tool.

What do you do when you have a good rain? You dig a deeper hole at one end and then dig a trench around the bottom of the hole, and sleep in your poncho. When the deeper hole starts to fill with water you bail it out using your steel helmet. What did we use for a pillow? We used either our arm or our steel helmet. In the winter we wore a loosely woven wool hat under our steel helmet and its associated-but-independent liner. The wool hat buffered the cold, hard, steel a bit when the helmet was being used as a pillow.

If your hole has a cover, as mentioned earlier, you may cover the entrance with a poncho, but someone has to keep look out. The rule on standing guard was 1 hour on and 1 hour off. If it was a three-man hole, you got to sleep two hours. This routine was followed every night, and was considered SOP (Standard Operating Procedure) as long as we were in combat. If we were told to dig in following a ditch line or in a ditch, we dug clumps out of the sides of the ditch and made two walls; the deeper the ditch, the higher the walls. A shallow ditch called for digging down first and then making walls. Some days I recall, we walked all day in the rain and then finished it off by digging a hole through the mud. We weren't called mudsloggers for nothing! In the winter, we chipped through the frozen top layer of ground and after that it was ordinary digging.

Ace: *Did you wipe your feet before you got back in here?*

Slick: *You find me a dry place and I will.*

During the war a paper was published by the military, called the Stars and Stripes. The paper was distributed both in the Pacific and European Theaters of Operation. Each issue had a cartoon in which two characters always appeared, Willie and Joe. The cartoon was called "Up Front with Bill Mauldin" and was written and drawn by Bill Mauldin. The cartoons were always funny, and truly typical in portraying bits of life of a pair of Dogfaces on line. Willie and Joe were always unshaven, dirty, and grubby looking. In winter they wore overcoats and in the summer they wore the standard fatigue jackets. (Some outfits wore overcoats but my outfit rejected them because when they got wet, they weighed a ton, and it seemed that they stayed wet all the time.)

James Whitmore, the actor, was a marine in WWII, and appeared as a consultant in a TV program about life in the military. He made this choice comment about Mauldin's Willie and Joe: "Those two guys were so real I could smell them, that's right, I could smell them."

Anyway, I have thrown in a couple of cartoons to give the reader a taste of what we looked forward to, relished, and enjoyed. There was a lot of other news in the Stars and Stripes, which we eagerly read, being news-starved the way we were.

STORIES RELATED TO HOLES

I mentioned earlier about our Piper Cub spotter calling in our own artillery on us. Soon after that, we stopped in the woods and dug in, in a ditch. We knew the Germans were near. This time, four of us dug three walls so we had two holes end-to-end adjoining. We had covers (because we were in the woods) and the openings of our holes were adjoining. When the guy in the next hole stood up and I stood in mine, we faced each other, with a dirt wall between. Our line was very erratic as opposed to a straight line going through the wood. The Germans broke through our line, somewhere to the left of the area that my platoon was in. The Germans were now in front, behind and to the left of us. Our platoon CP (command post) was behind us. The CP got hit by a roaming enemy party and managed to dispatch the roamers.

Reference note: A platoon's CP, personnel-wise, consisted of a lieutenant, platoon guide, platoon runner, radioman, and medic.

Since we didn't know from which direction a threat might come, our adjoining hole buddies, while standing watch, looked to the rear and my buddy or I looked forward.

I was doing just that when the guy I was facing gave me a frantic hand signal to get down. Now like I said, he was facing the rear. I bent my knees and crouched down. He had a BAR (Browning automatic rifle) that could fire 15 rounds automatically, or push a lever and fire them semi-automatically. He had the end (the business end) of the BAR right over the top of my helmet. I put my fingers in my ears and he squeezed the trigger, in the auto mode. He killed three Germans about fifteen feet away. Like I said, they didn't know exactly where we were, and vice versa.

That night was a bit tense. I stood guard, as mentioned before, one hour on and one hour off, with my dig-in mate. Since we didn't know how close or from what direction the enemy might come, we looked and strained our ears for the slightest sound. The more you did this kind of thing, the more you became like an animal in the wild. Anyway, I stood guard with my M1 in my left hand, safety off, and my right hand free in case a grenade came from the direction of some of that noise. Fun, fun. More gray hair and more promises to the Almighty.

Another time, I was alone in a slit trench just inside the edge of a wooded area. We had dug in after dark and the ground was stony and full of roots. It had rained during most of the night and when I awakened, my left hand, which had been exposed to the rain, was white and wrinkled. I had a dishpan hand! (Be good to me and don't ask how much guard I stood that night.) A short while later, I took my poncho off and laid it outside, just at the edge of the hole. It was on the side of the hole furthest from the Germans, or if you like, I was between the Germans and the poncho. The enemy saw some movement on our side, so they sent over a couple of good morning artillery shells. They hit close. Afterwards, I checked my poncho and it had shrapnel holes in it. My hole was quite shallow and I never will understand how that shrapnel got by me and through the poncho.

Ace: *Those damn Kraut shells are getting closer and closer. What if one caves our hole in?*

Slick: *I dunno, I guess we'll have to dig up!*

Ace: *Where do you throw the dirt when you dig up?*

Slick: *I dunno again, why don't ya write and ask your congressman? He's the one that put us here.*

ANOTHER HOLE STORY

On this particular day, we moved out of our holes first thing in the morning. In single file, we strung out and hiked forward. We advanced maybe a mile when the familiar command was heard, "Spread out and dig in." I remember the frequency of events that day, making it easy to remember the sequence. One of the guys and I dug a nice deep hole as the ground was good for digging and the weather was nice. With the hole done, now was the time to eat breakfast. As we started to open a box of breakfast K-rations, intending on a nice leisurely repast, the familiar words broke the stillness of the mid-morning air, "Saddle up, we're moving out."

Leaving the hole we had just dug, which was at the edge of an airfield, we moved about a quarter of a mile to the other side of the field and then spread out and dug in again. Once again the ground was good for digging so we dug an even bigger and nicer hole. We were able to scrounge around for some straw that was nearby and put it in the bottom of the hole, and as luck would have it there was a big stack of doors nearby. One of the doors made a quick cover for the hole and with some loose dirt shoveled on it we were doing just fine. Hell, we could stay in this hole until the war ends. With our "hole" security taken care of we could finally build a small fire, heat some water for instant coffee, and get to eating that late breakfast. Then along came (you guessed it): "Saddle up, we're moving out."

Now was the time for some therapeutic Army-style swear words. It didn't make any difference who or what they were directed at, just let them fly. Shit, it wasn't noon yet and we had dug two queen size, burial depth holes and we hadn't had a bite to eat or a sip of coffee. Yeah, I know, "We should have dug faster!" and "Go tell your troubles to the chaplain, if you can find one!"

We moved forward again and I don't think we were really out of sight of the last holes we had dug, when once again, "Spread out and [you know the words]." I will not say I was angry, as that is civilian talk. I was Army-style pissed off, big time, and said, "I don't give a damn, I'm not digging another hole just to move out after it's done." While all the other guys started digging slowly and with reluctance, I sat on the ground and sullenly watched.

We weren't there long at all when, wouldn't you know it, the enemy artillery decided to send us greetings. Their calling cards were way too close for my bodily comfort. That was the first time I tried digging a hole while lying on my side. You know, it's slow digging but you can make progress. Their artillery quieted down and I returned to digging normally. There was a lesson to be learned that day: when a person is really motivated, a sudden change of mind can be brought about!

Later they fired off about a dozen mortar shells. We heard and counted the distinctive cough of them being fired, but none of them exploded.

Reference note: We counted mortar shells as a defensive measure. If we counted them being fired and then heard each one hit or exploding, then we knew that that particular danger had passed.

AIRPLANES / PATTON

Planes

The strategic bombing carried out by our Air Force was the biggest single thing that contributed to the Allied victory. You might ask here, "well what about the people back home building airplanes, tanks, and all the rest of the war supplies?" and you would be right. WITHOUT THE WAR SUPPLIES, ALL WOULD HAVE BEEN LOST. Both the Japanese and the Germans made one of their biggest mistakes in underestimating the U.S.'s ability to convert our industrial plants from peacetime production to a war materials-producing colossus. What I am addressing is the combat or fighting aspect of the war. The Air Force knocked out the enemy's oil supplies first, ball bearing production second, and military targets third. I believe that I read the figure of 12 percent of all casualties incurred by the American forces in Europe were from the Air Force. Prior to the invasion, the Air Force had gained air superiority. The Germans used up their experienced air personnel in trying to stop the air raids. The German Luftwaffe could not train new pilots fast enough to attain a seasoned force. Their young pilots just didn't last long enough to gain real experience.

The American fighter pilots were something else. With air superiority, they were able to bomb and strafe anything that moved. Their only deterrent was the weather. Not long after the beachhead had been established, the guideline became: "When the German planes come over, the British and Americans get into their holes. When the British planes come over, the Germans get into their holes. When the American planes came over, everyone gets into their holes!" For a while, anything on the ground that moved was fair game. During this early period, we had a U.S. plane fly over and strafe us. Our ack-ack shot him down. Some of our guys went out and rescued the pilot. When the pilot crash-landed he had broken a leg. One reason the ack-ack got on him so quickly was that he was by himself. Usually, they ran around in fours. That particular pilot was probably just cruising, looking for any target of opportunity.

Word spread and communication between air and ground improved. A little later, a remedy was conceived on how to define Allied force's ground positions versus the enemy's. Orange banners, or flat pieces of orange cloth, were distributed. When an Allied aircraft attacked, mistakenly, our forces put the cloth on the hood of a jeep or truck and ran it into the center of a field. It was highly visible from the air and was effective.

One time I was in the middle of a field obeying nature's call. A British Spitfire, flying low, dropped a bomb near us. I headed for the nearest ditch while a jeep with its banner was brought into action. Needless to say, I beat the jeep by a mile. We found out later that when the Brit tried to release his bomb, it hung up on its release mechanism. When it did drop, it was over us. Still, uncivilized of that Brit, really, catching me in the field that way!

Another time we were dug in, in a long straight line. In front, the land sloped down into a valley. Once again, we were strategically positioned on the high ground. A lone enemy pursuit plane (Me 109) circled over once, then dropped down to fly over our line. It was broad daylight and he was flying from our right to left. Someone on our far right fired a single shot. Just past us, he started trailing smoke and I think he went down. One shot. Good shooting, yes!

Patton

Later in the afternoon at the same location, General George Patton and his entourage in three jeeps paid us a visit. About fifty yards to the left of the hole I was in was a blacktop road running perpendicular to our line of defense. All three vehicles stopped at our line of defense, one behind the other, and all personnel piled out. It reminded me of the President of the United States exiting a vehicle, with all of his bodyguards moving to see who can get closest to him. Patton started walking forward, looked to his left, and stopped. There was a light machine gun dug in about ten yards from the road. Patton walked over to the hole and said, "How come you don't have any camouflage on this hole? You know, it's soldiers like you that we have to write home about and say we regret to inform you that your Oscar is missing in action." Back on the road and followed by his staff, he walked further into Jerry-land. He scanned the area with BIG binoculars, and then headed back. "Oscar" had put some branches around his hole and when Patton walked back, he walked over and told him, "That's better."

When it came to dress, you have never seen a more soldierly looking soldier than Gen. George S. Patton. He was spit and polish to the nth degree. His helmet and boots looked like they were in a race to see which could outshine the other. He was tall and broad shouldered and his clothes were tailored to accentuate his shape. His orderly, the one taking care of his clothes, was doing a fine job. I add this for laughs: one time a chaplain asked him if he ever prayed, to which Patton replied, "Every goddamn night." According to his book, he did pray, and read the Bible nightly. Patton and his Third Army were responsible for taking probably the lion's share of all captured or liberated ground in Sicily, France, and Germany. He was hell on wheels and highly respected by the Germans.

When he spearheaded the run after the breakout in Normandy, they asked him, "What are you going to do about your flanks if you just push forward?" He said, "To hell with my flanks, I'll push and kick their asses so fast and hard they will never get organized enough to hit back."

His tactics had never been tried before in the history of warfare, but they were successful. My division was assigned to Patton and his Army at the time of the breakthrough out of the hedgerows in Normandy. We traveled, on foot, in support of the tanks and as I recall, we walked twenty miles a day for seven days straight trying to keep up with Patton's armor. We still had to dig in at night and we ate nothing but K-rations. Even with spare socks, my feet started bleeding from wet, sweaty socks. They stayed dirty because we were never in a spot where water was available for washing. Finally an available stream was there at the end of a day. With freshly washed and dried socks, my feet responded favorably and I was able to keep going.

Another incident that was related to our strolling across the roads and fields of France had to do with our Army-issued (what other kind were there?) boxer shorts. Hiking had a tendency to make the legs on our shorts bunch up, moving them up to our limit, the groin. The next thing you knew this area started to get raw. The idea then became to pin down the bottom of the shorts to prevent them from riding up. If you didn't have and couldn't find or borrow a pin to hold the shorts down, you dealt with the hurt. So, using a field-expedient alternative, we sharpened a small stick and shoved it through both pants and shorts. Don't laugh, it worked!

I don't know if it was during one of these promenades or not, but the sole on Joe Lopez's shoe had come unstitched. As he walked he had to flip his foot out so the sole would be flat when he put the foot down. Most poor kids, raised during the Depression, know exactly what that loose flapping sole feels and acts like. Joe had reported it but nothing had been done. Well, he was flip-flopping along one day when the Regimental Commander, Colonel Warren A. Robinson, came by in a jeep. He spotted flip-flop Joe. The colonel stopped and talked to Joe. Three days later, Joe had a new set of boots delivered, and they were the right size.

Planes and Rockets

We were traveling along in a convoy of trucks. I don't know how many guys to a truck, but we always traveled standing room only. The convoy came to a screeching halt. German planes were in the air. The driver of the truck we were in peeled out of the truck and dashed alongside and around the back of the truck. To the right of the road we were on was a ditch, a small clearing, then a wooded area. The driver was heading for the woods. When he rounded the back of the truck, he picked up speed and jumped that ditch in one long stride. Afterward, we checked out the width of the ditch. Even though we saw him jump it, we just couldn't believe it. I'm sure unofficial history in the broad jump had just been made (and that guy didn't land on two feet but had taken it in stride). Aside from the driver, there must have been something going on to our right rear, as there were antiaircraft guns there. Four enemy planes came by, one by one, with a decent gap between them. The ack-ack went after them. They turned, trailed smoke, and went down, all four. Once again, good shooting.

We were on line long enough to see the first German jets go by. They flew low and fast. They were something like the German 88s in that you heard their noise and before you could react, they were already overhead and going through. This was especially true if you were in any kind of a valley when they flew over. We also saw the German V-1 or V-2 rockets, earlier in the campaign. For those unfamiliar with what V-1s and V-2s were, the letter V stood for "vengeance," as named by the Germans. Most of us called them Buzz Bombs and a lot of the British called them Doodlebugs. They were rocket-propelled bombs that had short wings to add stability to their flight. They used a gyrocompass system for height and wind correction control. Today, we are used to seeing rockets being fired straight up, but these rockets were launched at, let's say, a forty-five degree angle, destination London, England. You might say they were launched on a giant arch that was flat in its mid-path, from Germany to London. The rocket terminated its forward flight when the time on a preset timer ran out. It would be buzzing along, and the preset timer would time out, shutting the fuel off. A mechanical switch would kick in, changing the equivalent of ailerons on the wings, causing the rocket to go quiet and change its trajectory, pointing towards the ground, explosive end first. Its accuracy (as far as landing on its intended target, London) was determined primarily by the amount of time set on its timer. The first few rockets sent each day included a radio signal transmitter, which the Germans triangulated with signal detectors. They would then know how much the wind conditions affected the total flight time, allowing them to readjust the following rockets' timers, in hopes of hitting the center of London. They launched approximately 8,000 V-1s and about 2,500 actually landed on London. Each rocket carried about a ton of explosives. The rockets' range was around 150-160 miles, so they were fired from outside Calais, France, which is located right on the other side of the English Channel. The difference between the number of rockets fired and the number not getting to the target was due to the effectiveness of British antiaircraft, British pursuit planes shooting them down, and the antiaircraft balloons that were in the air. British Spitfire pursuit planes were also known to intercept the rockets short of their intended target, fly alongside and maneuver their wing tip under the wing tip of one of the rockets, lift the rocket's wing tip, disturbing the rocket's forward flight and sending it into the ground. The V-1 was the first "cruise missile."

The V-2 rocket was a true high arch rocket, and at the top of its flight path it was on the fringe of outer space. Its speed in flight attained 3,500 miles per hour. There were 1,000 launched and about half managed to land on target. Their payload was also about 1600 pounds of explosives.

The Germans also developed a V-3 rocket that was small and was fired from a cannon. The system was designed such that they could send the V-3s in waves of 300 rockets per hour. Allied bombers, using massive bombs on the well-fortified launching sites, curtailed the effectiveness of the V-3s, reducing their use to next to nothing.

One other minor point on planes: Within three days after the invasion of Normandy, an airstrip was being built in the American sector.

REST AND DRINKING

I read in *The Cross Of Lorraine, A Combat History Of The 79th Infantry Division* that the 79th Division went 127 days in combat with no formal rest. That covered the time from their first action at Cherbourg through the action at the Forest of Parroy. During those 127 days, at least while I was with them, we may have spent three or an exceptional four days in any one particular place; it was always in a hole, on night guard, and on the same rations. The divisional history book says that when we did go on rest, the men slept in beds in the rest area in the town of Luneville. My platoon, and probably my whole company, slept on the dirt floor of an old factory building. We were there sixteen days. I personally didn't give a damn what we slept on, as long as we were off line. Even in the rest area, kitchen food was short and was supplemented with K-rations. We did have a change of clothes and left looking like green troops. While we were in the rest area, we were allowed to order some bottles of champagne as a special treat. Another guy and I decided to split a bottle. When it was delivered, we sat around a fire we had made on the dirt floor and drank. It was the first time I ever tasted champagne. I drank my half of the bottle and wondered what the big deal about champagne was. Then I laid back on my blankets and went to sleep.

Much earlier, there was another time when drinking entered the picture. It was during the summer and we had not received our water ration for the day. We were on a road and we came under direct fire from an 88. Our defense was to run like hell until the 88 couldn't see us anymore. We were running in small groups past a clearing while moving down the road and then waiting for the rest to catch up. I was laying on the ground, alongside the road, when I noticed some water in the ditch. The water had a green slime on the surface. I carefully made an opening in the slime and filled my canteen. We carried Listerine tablets with us. They were supposed to kill all the bad guys in the water, after maybe a couple of hours. I gave it a short fifteen minutes. It tasted fine. At the next break, someone said, "McDonnell's got water." I explained to them how and where the water came from. No matter, in double-swig time it was gone. A positive thought at the time was, if I have to go back with food poisoning, I wouldn't be alone. It may have been that cheese, sticking to the sides of the stomach, that immunized us. Score one for the cheese? No way.

One more short shot on drinking: Toward the end of the war, a plan was initiated whereby personnel would be sent to a rest center for three days. My turn came and I was more than elated to head out and back. When I got to the rest center it was wall-to-wall GIs and no one seemed to have anywhere to go. I told myself that I can do better than this, so I hitchhiked back to Holland and stayed with the same people whose house I lived in while taking amphibious training, prior to crossing the Rhine River. My whole company had been billeted in that village, two or three guys to each house. My host family was very happy to see me and treated me royally. Word spread that I was there and as I walked through the village people would come out and inquire about this guy or that one, always wanting to know if the soldier was alive and well. I had more invitations to afternoon tea and cookies than I could handle.

When I got back to my platoon, a prohibition law had been passed. It seems that while going house to house, cleaning out the German soldiers, the platoon came across some houses with well-supplied wine cellars. Enough guys got crocked that a sufficient guard couldn't be mustered. A direct order was issued to all, "NO MORE DRINKING."

THIS TIME, THE REAL THING

On this particular mission we moved up and into what had been, possibly, a slave labor camp, complete with barracks and barbed wire fencing. Outside the camp was a long hill made out of what appeared to be slack coal. On the other side of the long hill was a water canal, which separated us from some Krauts that we could see on the other side. I wasn't feeling good, so I went in one of the barracks and laid on one of the bunk beds. My squad was up on the top of the long pile, taking pot shots at the enemy. Shortly, one of the guys came in the barracks. He had his helmet in his hand. He said, "I've had enough of that shit, look." His helmet had a nice clean bullet crease in it. One of the Germans probably had a scope on his rifle. Well, I started getting sicker and began emptying out, both ends. The last I remember of those barracks, I was on a stretcher being slid through a window. The medics used that route as it was less exposed than the door—they probably backed right up to it with their jeep or whatever.

The next thing I knew I was on my back in a hospital and a doctor was leaning over me. I heard him say, "He'll be alright, he's coming around now." To this day, I don't know what I had eaten, assuming it was food poisoning, nor how long I was actually "out."

Talking about the German using a scope back at the canal reminds me of something. Early on in combat, we had a guy in our platoon that was a designated sniper. He carried a 1903 thirty caliber bolt-action rifle with a scope on it. One time I saw how effective he and the rifle were. We were on high ground with a bowl-shaped valley to the front. One guy was walking at the bottom of the valley and looked like he was about as tall as your index finger, at that distance. Someone sent for Larry and his sniper rifle. He looked through his scope and said, "Yeah, it's a German." He took his time and squeezed one off. We could see the guy go down. Did the German hear the bullet and fake it? I don't know. I do know that when it was Larry's turn to meet his maker, he got it in the forehead. Another sniper? I told you earlier about crossing the river with the dog, getting a piece of hot stuff in the back, crossing the railroad tracks and then into the woods. Well, when we got into the woods at that spot, the lieutenant, Larry, and one other guy went on a short reconnoiter. Two of them returned shortly, and the one left in the woods was Larry. They told us how it happened: just one shot, they had looked down at Larry and saw where he had been hit in the head, and then they skedaddled.

CAUGHT SLEEPING AGAIN

One time back in the summer, we were walking on a blacktop road, a column on each side of the road and ten paces between each man. There was a clearing on each side of the road, then wooded area. I was walking on the left side of the road and there was a ditch to my left, maybe eight to ten feet from me. The front of the column, a half of a city block up ahead of me, was approaching a crossroad.

All at once, a machine gun, from the far side of the crossroad, opened up on us. The name of the game at this point was, take cover, posthaste. I took two paces left and dove for the ditch. You won't believe my luck. I landed smack dab on top of a mattress that was lying in the ditch. I never saw it until I was in the air.

To the best of my knowledge, that German didn't hit anyone. We wondered at the time, "What the hell was coming down? You were not supposed to be walking in a column of twos into the enemy." Facts be known, that guy on the machine gun must have been asleep. Strange!

ANOTHER STRANGE

Night Attack

We were dug in one evening and after dark, we were told to saddle up. It seems some joker had made the decision that a night attack was the right way to go. We moved out and after passing through and between houses, we hit a clearing, then more houses, left to right, and a road beyond and parallel to the houses, beyond the road, woods. We got near the houses when things came alive. There were Germans in the woods on the other side of the road just waiting for company. The second platoon (my platoon) was hoping there would be nobody at home. Before we had a chance to ring any doorbells the Germans greeted us with a machine gun and other small arms fire. I went with a couple of guys into the house, then on up to the second floor. Go to the high ground and see where they are and give it to them from on high, right? Well not so fast, they had that figured too.

We took the first shots on our part and they countered with an antitank round. It hit about a foot from the window frame on the outside. The resulting part of the house flying around missed us, so we went in the next bedroom. We waited for the next blast, but that gun crew was playing fair. They wanted us to have another turn first.

Time hung heavy and all grew quiet. We agreed that one of the guys would go down and see what was going on. He came back up and said, "Everyone's gone," meaning our guys. I told them to go and take a good look and I would hold still. They left and never came back. Then, "bullshit," I decided to leave too. I headed back to the area we had started from. I knew guards would be out and nervous, maybe expecting a follow through counterattack. We didn't have a password for the day. I got the idea of making noise as I moved along, so I kept snapping the gum I was chewing. I was in the habit of making "that noise" as I chewed the one stick in each K-ration, and the guys around me knew it. Sure 'nuff, two guards picked up the gum noise, and before seeing them I heard, "McDonnell, is that you?"

It was real crazy that night. One of the guys in my squad walked right on out into Jerry-land and upon returning told quite a story. He had come face to face with a German and both being surprised, both did an about face and ran. Another guy, showing up the next morning, told of how he had gotten lost, found some wine, and gotten drunk. (This was before company prohibition.) This particular guy got drunk real easy. From past experiences, we used to say that if you slapped him in the ass with a rotten apple, he'd be drunk. We never did find out if he got that bottle before or after the attack. Night attacks! What a way to get fouled up.

I don't know if it was in the same place or not but the next day's ration party was going back for water and K's, and once again, in the dark. We were told that the tankers were sitting on the edge of town to our rear and to watch out for them, as they were trigger happy.

Animals

Let's back up a bit. After being in combat a while, your sense of hearing, direction, and smell become keener.

You condition yourself to react to different sounds. As soon as you hear the first sound of a shell, you categorize it for degree of threat and react immediately. Whose rifle just fired? If it's enemy machine gun or rifle fire, how far away and in which direction? A mortar being fired, wait to see where it is going to hit. A Screaming Mimi, or a concussion rocket, means possible concussion, so cover your ears. To give you an idea of what a Screaming Mimi is like, I can compare it to one of the rockets they send up at the Fourth of July fireworks. The personnel in charge of the fireworks fire the rocket high in the air and when it goes off it has a record setting, for the night, boom. The sound is not only extra loud but the chest can feel the pressure wave from the explosion. Now instead of the rocket exploding way up in the air, have it go off on the ground somewhere in your near vicinity. Yeah, cover your ears and I'm forgetting, open your mouth, too. All of this categorizing of sounds becomes automatic. A cricket at night was a good sound. When it stopped its noise, you listened harder. When most anything moves around a cricket, including a man, the cricket goes silent.

Our sense of smell was also improved, being outside all the time. When we moved into an area that the Germans had evacuated, there was a distinctive smell. If it was an enclosed dug out, the smell was stronger. If we were attacking and moving into the wind, I would smell the air. If I smelled them, they were there or there were signs they had been there. Our sense of smell wasn't as keen as a dog's or a bear's, but we kept trying.

Ernie Pyle was right in more ways than one, "We lived like animals." We dug and lived in the ground like moles, wallowed in mud and stayed as dirty as pigs, ate food at times that a dog wouldn't, never bathed unless it rained real hard, defecated in the field, and sniffed the air like any other well developed animal.

OK, we're going back for rations in the dark and have been warned that there are tankers behind us and they may be trigger happy. We were inside a town and following a board fence and there was a small barn on our immediate right. There was also the faintest silhouette of a house to our front and the wind was blowing with sporadic gusts. All at once, there was this loud fluttering "whoooo" noise and it was right on top of us. We froze and the hair on the back of my neck stood up. I don't know if there is such a thing as double freeze or not. If there is, we did, and held it like, "Don't move and don't make a sound." The thing was, we had never heard that sound before. It was a completely new sound, and so our immediate reaction was fear. All at once it did it again. It was some loose tin on the roof of the shed, being rattled by the wind. It took a bit for our nerves to settle and the rest of the trip was cautious but uneventful.

Instincts

A word on instincts: I believe there are animal instincts in all of us. Being raised or living in a "civilized" home, town, or society, those instincts don't have a chance to develop. A person living in the wild and being exposed to dangers takes on or develops some of our latent instincts. We really never know what our bodies and minds are capable of until they are put to the test. It is good to know our "limits" are higher than we thought they would be, but then again, what is the price one has to pay to find out?

THE BREAK'S OVER

It was around mid-October and the divisional rest period was over. When we left the area, we were dressed for winter, having donned long underwear, tops and bottoms, cotton boxer shorts, undershirt, two pairs of pants, wool shirt, wool sweater, fatigue jacket, wool cap, extra socks, wool gloves, and boot packs on our feet. The boot packs were rubber on the bottom to just below the ankles then leather half way up the calf of the leg. I think the insole was felt. We were told that if the boot packs were laced to the top and then laced around the top and tied, they would be watertight. That sounded good and even glamorous. In truth, if you walked any distance, the boot got so warm that the feet started to sweat. The feet sweat so much that after a good hike you could remove your socks and wring the sweat out. We always slept with our boots on and during the night the cold would penetrate from the rubber through to the wet socks. The boots did not fill the bill for walkers and we were infantry, by definition and action.

The night we left the rest area, we wound up just behind the artillery, as they were booming to the front of us. And then something odd started happening. Every now and then a rifle went off along our line. There were too many to be just someone discharging his rifle accidentally. After all was said and done, it seems some were shooting themselves, rather than face more of the same. The fact that they had been so safe for a while and were now having to go back into hell was more than some could take. Most didn't realize that a self-inflicted wound was easy for the doctors to spot and the doctors were under orders to report all self-inflicted wounds.

I never tried to pass judgment on self-shooters. Anyone who has been in the thick of it will weigh different means of getting out of it, including desertion. There were exceptions, but I'll say that most who have been there for any length of time considered deeply what it would cost to get out. For some, the thought that their time is up and they are going to get it became obsessive. About the time of my poncho getting shrapnel holes in it, one of the guys asked me to take off with him. I told him I didn't figure my time was up. He stayed and held out for quite a bit longer, but he did die in action.

I don't know if it was the night we slept behind the artillery, or the next night, but I awakened with an inch of snow on my blanket. Our night amenities were nothing to brag about in the positive sense, negative yes, but not positive. The usual fare was one Army blanket, single bed size, per man, regardless of the weather. Sometimes when we received the blanket it was frozen. We would literally peel the rolled blanket open, get under or in it, and go to sleep. I say in it, as the blanket was wide enough, if you folded it once and slid between the fold, it would just cover you on both sides. If we spent the day in one spot we would stay wrapped in a blanket when it was really cold out. How cold? I would guess the coldest to be around zero F. Most of the time, like I have said before, we buddied up on holes and one stood guard while the other slept. The guard usually wrapped himself in his blanket. But I'll tell you, a well dug hole with branches, dry leaves, dry grass, or hay bottom, and a cover on the hole, could be comfortable. Building a small fire to cook or dry your socks could make it hot in the hole. Most of the time, though, we didn't sit still long enough to have the concierge arrange our holes to take on the airs of a presidential suite. Amen to that.

BOOT PACK / TRENCH FOOT

We were less than a month out of the rest center when one morning I crawled out of my hole, stood up, and found my feet wouldn't support me. I crawled back in the hole and took my boots and socks off. My socks were still wet and my feet were an anemic white and wrinkled. The cold and wet had gotten to them and they suffered from lack of circulation. My spare socks were no better, so I opened a K-ration and used the box for a fire. Holding the socks over it, I got some of the moisture out. I massaged my bare feet to get the circulation going and then I was able to stand up. This was the beginning of trench foot. The first and second stages are, no circulation, then loss of feeling and control. The third stage is when gangrene sets in and the only cure for it is amputation. I was into the first stage. The other time sleeping in the rain I had a dishpan hand, now it was dishpan feet. This is the result of the skin being soaked in water too long. Like I said, those boot packs were not all that wonderful for the infantry. A word or two on trench foot later, when I wind up in a hospital.

ZOMBIE

Just prior to the incident where I couldn't stand up on my feet in my foxhole, I had started to act like a zombie. (I'll discuss the word "zombie" later.) Anyway, we were walking single file through a very long snow-covered field. I can't be too sure of its length because it was quite a while back, but I'll guess it was a quarter mile long. The field had splotches of black, the telltale sign of where artillery shells had hit. The only other thing that disturbed that beautiful clean white field of snow was the trail laid down by a single file of my outfit moving forward. A few lone shells came in as we moved forward through the field and everyone hit the ground. Except me: I was of the frame of mind that I didn't care if I got hit or not, so I stayed standing. Ahead of us, at the end of the field, was a road that ran from right to left, raised above the field by three to five feet. Straight ahead and to our left on the road were two houses, face to face. They were the last two houses on the end of a small settlement or village. Just as I was getting to the edge of the road, I heard a shell with payday on it. My experienced ear told me this sound means "you are in trouble." Instinct and self-preservation took over, and I barreled ass across the road, getting the house on the far side of the road between danger and me. By the sound, that shell couldn't have been more than six feet higher than the road. After the area where my feet showed a lack of cooperation, we moved out and my platoon got wiped out, yours truly included. But before I get into that, I want to share another incident.

Shit List

I think this incident came about more toward the end of winter. We were loaded on trucks and told that we were moving back. Rumor (and I repeat, rumor) had it that we were going for regimental reorganization, and that meant rest. Hot dog! Partway back, the trucks stopped, turned around, and continued forward. New rumor: A new division on line had been hit and broken through by the enemy, and our services were needed. "Oh shit and pukesville." The trucks came to their "we go no further point" and we unloaded and headed through the woods. After a mile or so through a wooded area, we came to a road that ran left to right. Along the ditch on our approach side to the road lay dead Germans. To the right, on both sides of the road, the tree line ended and there was open ground for maybe 60 yards, then another tree line and woods.

I think I was the last man of my platoon coming up and had not crossed the road. Our lieutenant, a new man, moved out into the opening with a few men, looked back and saw me. He yelled, "What the hell are you doing over there?" I answered, "I'm trying to keep contact with the platoon behind," which was the right thing to do in the woods. He yelled, "Get your ass over here." Right about then, small arms fire broke out. I went back to the tree line and crossed the road, which was elevated with shallow ditches on either side. In the deep gully-like depression perpendicular to the road lay more dead GIs and a few wounded Americans, from the other division, who couldn't walk. This gully was deep enough to kneel in and have your head level with the ground. My squad had followed the gully and was swapping fire with the Germans stationed in the tree line on the far side of the clearing. My guess would be that our guys were no more than 50 yards from the road.

The lieutenant and a few others were in the clearing, among the knee-high bushes and weeds. The lieutenant, lying flat and hidden in the bushes, called out to me, and I moved out towards him. He told me that he wasn't able to raise the captain on his walkie-talkie and that I should go back and see if I could find someone. Rising up and thereby exposing myself, I ran to the gully and then the road. I saw nothing. I crawled back to the looie and reported, "I can't see no one." At this time, a German came out of the woods directly in front of us. He saw us, and wheeled back around before anyone could shoot. I asked if anyone had a grenade launcher, and we fired a white phosphorous grenade up into the top of the trees. All was quiet.

Then the looie told me to go back across the road and try to find someone. This time I dropped my gear, including my M1, and picked up someone else's carbine. I stood up again, exposing myself again, and headed for the gully. This time, the Germans tried chasing me with an antiaircraft gun. That would be one twin, 20 mm, rapid-fire, aerial-bursting motivator. I probably didn't set a world record for short spurt, but I tried. Once I was inside the tree line, the ack-ack gunner gave up. Before crossing, I wondered if maybe those German jokers were now covering the road. I looked for a culvert that might run under the road, so I could avoid exposure on the road. Nope, no culvert, so I made a dash across the road and into the woods. I looked high and low and found no one. I retraced my steps and when I got back in the gully, looking across the brush clearing, I could see our guys inside the woods with the looie. I picked up my gear on the way over and when I got there, there were six

German prisoners with them. The looie said, "Someone has to take these guys back." He looked around and when he looked at me, I looked him straight in the eyes. He said, "You do it." In the Army this is a perfect example of being on the looie's "shit list." To myself, "Sweet shit, how am I going to move these guys through that same clearing?"

Prisoners

I took them onto the road in plain sight, lined them up and marched them out. I walked with one guy in close on my immediate right. Using the German as a shield, my thought was that if anyone got me, it would have to be a sniper or better. At the same time, I wanted to show their buddies farther down in the woods that some were surrendering. Halfway through that clearing, they sent an artillery shell over. It hit close enough. Have you ever had the experience of looking at a particular spot on a lake and seeing a fish jump out of the water? Well, that was the way with me. I was looking at one of the German's upper sleeve, and I saw this black spot appear: a piece of shrapnel from that shell had hit him.

We moved forward and into the woods and along the same path my platoon had followed coming up there. The guy that got hit was falling behind. He was tall and acted like a baby, with a lot of self-sympathy. I had another prisoner walk with him so that he could try to help him. All of a sudden, Jerry came along and put a few shells in our path. They had that damn path zeroed in—they knew that any traffic coming or going would be along it. When the shell hit, my prisoners hit the ground—in fear. I didn't go down because I didn't want them to run on me. When they looked up and saw me standing, amazement and wonder showed on their faces.

I kept trying to hurry them up when a GI stepped out of the woods and told me to say "mock schnell" ("make speed" or "move faster"). With a new command in hand, we moved smoother. Big Fart with the wounded arm always stayed the same distance behind. His helper was now up with the rest of us.

When we got back to the line of the divisional people we were helping out, one of their guards rose up very excitedly, and with his M1 pointing at us he said, "Get away from them ... get away!" I was carrying the carbine by my side, walking beside the prisoners. I told the guard, "Lower that rifle." He didn't, and then repeated what he had said before. This time I said, "I told you to put down that goddamn rifle," and then in a softer voice, "These guys aren't going anywhere." Slow Ass caught up with us and I had them all sit on the ground.

The group that had been overrun had a command post right there, dug in underground even, but would not relieve me of the prisoners. They called for transportation, and a jeep came up. We loaded all six prisoners into the jeep and took them farther back. I spent the night back there, sleeping inside a house on a nice dry floor with no guard duty. This was a self-allotted fringe benefit for chasing prisoners. I had my own one-day reorganization rest period (which is to say that I screwed off for a day where it was safe and quiet).

I hitchhiked a ride back next day, and climbed in with a couple of guys that had a big hole. The looie came around later and said, "I see you made it back." I said, "Yes, sir," and that was that. In retrospect I probably should have hunted the looie down to report myself back, but if he was in the same mood as when I left, he might have sent me out on a one-man patrol. About a month later, I was told that I was now a sergeant. I guess I did impress that looie. I also think that Joe Lopez had put in his two cents.

PLATOON WIPEOUT

The day after I had awakened, unable to stand on my feet, we were ordered to "saddle up!" before dawn. We walked a couple miles or more in the dark, until we came to a narrow river, not much more than a wide stream. Dawn was just breaking. It was November 18, 1944, and how well I remember it.

Beyond the river lay open ground for two to three hundred yards. At the far side of that was a six foot high embankment. Past the embankment were a railroad track and another six foot high embankment. From the second embankment, the field was open for at least seven hundred yards. To the right, the ground gradually sloped down for about one hundred yards. At the one hundred yard line was a farmer's three-strand barbed-wire fence, perpendicular to the railroad tracks. Immediately after the first fence, the ground dropped maybe eighteen inches to a lower level, then thirty to forty feet further was another three-strand barbed wire fence. At most fifty yards past the fence was a two-story house, and running close to it, a very long two-story barn.

We walked to the railroad tracks, and then up and to the top of the bank. We then formed a line of skirmishes, parallel to the fences, and maybe 100 yards from the first fence. Moving forward, we got to the position where about two thirds of the guys had crossed over the first barbed wire fence and were now in between the two fences. Then all hell broke loose and we were caught with our pants down.

Those of us that were between the two fences couldn't move forward or back. We were in a well-sprung trap. They had a machine gun on the left, rifles to our front, and to our far right was a rifleman. They were well camouflaged in their positions, we couldn't see them for squat, and in addition, they were so close they couldn't miss.

The field approaching and in between the barbed wire fences had 2 inch stubble on the ground. The fields had been plowed maybe a year before. The only hope for cover was to lie as flat as possible in the gullies between the furrows. That was no-where deep enough for us but we had to play our hand as well as we could, "depending on the situation and the terrain." The furrows ran parallel to the fences and you might say that "we were pinned down tighter than self-bonding paper." One guy tried to rush forward. He made it onto the barbed wire where the machine gun stopped him. As I said, we couldn't see where they were. One of the guys in my squad tried crawling forward and I yelled at him, "Don't crawl, make a short run." Crawling, as soon as his body was on the high point of the mound, he got shot. Then they dropped a couple of 60 mm mortar shells in on us. Just before that, I looked over and saw the medic kneeling beside a guy. After the mortar shells hit, I looked again and the medic was lying on top of the guy. For the Germans it was easy: if it moves, shoot it.

Our artillery tried putting a few smoke shells between the barbed wire and the house. Their accuracy was great, but the shells seemed to bury themselves and the amount of smoke emitted was like a burning cigarette lying there. The next thing, a German artillery piece, maybe a thousand yards away, on a high hill to our left, let loose. I don't know how that German artilleryman sighted his gun but he could have opened the breech and sighted along the inside of the barrel and decimated us. For some reason the shells hit close but not right on top of us.

Very shortly, four of our planes came over. I think someone from the ground contacted them. Lying flat, we could tell when the plane banked and started its dive. Let me tell you, when you are lying right under a plane, the roar of its engine keeps building and building and then the noise from its 50 cal. guns takes over. I could hear the slugs hitting the ground but in truth I didn't know if he was aiming at them or us. This was a new ass puckerer. One after another, they made a pass. We (I don't know how many were alive at this point) could only hug the ground and wait for the sound of the next plane to make its next dive. One of the planes tried dropping a five hundred pound bomb. It hit about two or three hundred yards away. I swear, when that bomb hit, the initial blast shook the ground and I bounced a foot in the air. It may have been six inches, but I know I went straight up and then gravity took over and I went back down.

I then decided that the only way I would get out of there was to go back. I figured I would get up and dive under the lowest strand of barbed wire as the ground level to my rear was eighteen inches higher than the ground I was on. I would throw my rifle over the top and roll with determination so that if my clothes hooked on a rusty old barb, I would tear free. I did it and it worked. Not bad for a guy who didn't care if he lived or not a couple of days ago. Motivation.

After a bit, I rose and made another short burst of a run. We had been taught it takes a rifleman a good three count before he can take aim. We weren't taught that the mud might build up on your boots and slow you down, which it was doing. When we covered that ground going to the fences the ground was hard but by the time I was making the return trip the morning sun was warming the ground to the point that the ground was getting muddy. I made another jump. I passed one of our guys who was lying there wounded. He rose up on all fours and started crawling to me. I raised my head and said, "Keep coming." Just as he was crawling into the furrow at my feet, they shot him again. I tried turning my head and looking under my armpit at him. He asked for water. Still lying as flat as possible, I snaked my canteen out of its pouch and threw it back to him. A minute later, I looked back and he looked white and out. In a little while, I picked my head up to look and one of those bastards put a round in the ground right in front of my nose. That ding-a-ling had been watching and waiting. He may have had a scope, but if he did the dummy jerked the trigger instead of squeezing it. The higher probability was that he had an ordinary open sighted rifle. I laid and played dead for a while. That German's ego told him he got me, and then maybe again he was low on ammo and wanted to make each shot count. Like so many other things, you'll never know.

[Don't be misled by how I am making light of it fifty and more years later: it was a deadly situation.]

My next run or two or three were the same. I was now maybe thirty yards from safety. I don't mean two points like in football, I mean my butt's safety. The next run I made, I decided to keep going until I heard a bang. I made it all the way to the railroad tracks.

When I got there, the guys, maybe twenty, were along the bank that was next to the open field. There were a couple of guys with a light machine gun and they were digging in furiously. That means some guys from a heavy weapons platoon had been attached to us. We must not have had any mortars, from the heavy weapons platoon, or they would have been brought into play. There was a looie there that I didn't know. Our own looie had bought it, so that left this other looie in command. I convinced him to try sending a few men along the tracks to get beyond the barbed wire. They moved out and didn't get far when small arms fire drove them back. The Germans must have had surveillance along that track. The Krauts knew their area of defense and had communications going. They were good.

They knew we were along and behind the bank, so they dropped mortar shells in on us. We could hear the cough as they were being fired as I explained before, and once again, we could hear them when they were maybe ten feet above the ground as they came in. I told you about my buddy Kraff earlier. He was right next to me when the first mortar round hit. We had taken up the fetal/sitting position up against the base of the bank. I had my arms folded alongside the exposed area of my neck and face. I kept my position after the shells had hit. I heard someone behind me say, "There's nothing we can do for him." I turned around. It was Kraff, the same guy that had survived so many near misses. A piece of shrapnel had hit him in the neck. He was gone.

The next round they put in, it was my turn. It hit me in the fleshy part of the right hip. Many times I had heard the involuntary noises or screams that fellow dogfaces had made upon being wounded. The screams that they made, to me, were demoralizing and I had made up my mind that if it happened to me, I would not scream. When shrapnel hits you, it is hotter than bejayses, and it burns like hell, so I tensed up, gritted my teeth, and waited for the burning to die down. In regard to strong will power: I have watched a fellow soldier get shot in the stomach, stop and put his hand over the wound, and then walk fifty more steps forward before dropping to the ground.

The next thing that happened was that artillery piece on the hill tried to get at us. No dice. As long as we were behind that bank, the only thing that could get us was the mortar and he wasn't able to see what his shells were doing.

After a while, things got quiet and a couple of the wounded walked across the open field toward the river. They carried their rifles by the sling with the rifle parallel to the ground. A couple more tried it. No rifle firing by the enemy. I headed back, doing the same thing, and still no firing by the enemy. I don't know if the Germans abandoned their positions before the wounded walked to the river or what, and I guess I'll never know.

Field Hospital

My next stop was the regimental field hospital. They put a tag on me and sent me back farther yet, via ambulance. I wound up in a full-fledged hospital and, as usual, was told the absolute minimum. In one room, they shaved me, and then back to a waiting room. I got a shot and was told it would make me drowsy so don't fall down. I was a non-critical walking patient, so I was left to near last for attention. I sat and read comic books. That was nice. Having lived outside all the time, I know my immunities were up and that shot had no more effect than a wet cigarette.

I was finally ushered into an operating room with two males in white; a female nurse was over in the corner. The one guy says, "Drop your pants." I hesitated, looking at the nurse in the corner. The guy in white says, "Don't mind her, if she hasn't seen it by now, it's time she had." Now, I had been going from before sun up, had had nothing to eat all day, and it was now probably around ten PM. I was wonderfully happy to be off line but hadn't thought to count my blessings as yet.

I started with pants one, then pants two, then long john bottoms, and before the shorts came down, the guy in white says, "You sure got enough clothes on." I answered, "Yeah, it's cold where I come from." Both of us were now off on the wrong foot. Guy in white: "Get on the table and turn on your left side." I did so and was in such a position that my left arm, bent at the elbow

190

was sticking out with the palm of my hand facing up. I felt him playing around at the wound and some fluid running down my front. Shortly he dropped the piece of shrapnel in my open palm and said, "Well, there it is." I looked at the bloody piece, and it was about the size of a thirty caliber slug, then turned my hand over and dropped it on the floor. I said, "I've seen bigger pieces." He asked, "You sorry you didn't get hit worse?" I replied, "You're damn right I am." He covered my wound and told me to go across the hall and wait in the room there. You know if he had told me who he was and what he was going to do, I would have known that he was a doctor and had more respect. In retrospect, I'm sure we were both at the end of a long day and both very tired.

A nurse came to get me and led me to a big ward and my assigned bed. I told her that I had yet to eat that day. She told me that the kitchen was closed but she would see what she could do. Now, you won't believe this, but she brought me a K-ration, and to top it off, it was a dinner ration with that lovely processed American cheese! Damn that cheese! I ate the ration, but not the cheese. The bed was super-wonderful—dry and warm. Happiness was mine! To this day, when I think of this, I give thanks that the bed I am in is warm and dry.

The next morning, a nurse came around and I asked her if I could have someone look at my feet, as I thought I had trench foot. She said, without a smile, "You'll have to wash them first." She told me where the bathroom was and where I could find a basin in the bathroom. I was performing said operation when a guy stuck his head in the door and said, "Are you McDonnell?" After a "yeah" on my part, he said "Get your things together, we're moving out," and he waited for me. My first thought was, "Shit, I'm going back." So I asked him, "Where are we headed?" He said, "Back to a general hospital." This time, with much enthusiasm, "Wonderful, let's go."

General Hospital

With my type of wound, the treatment was to leave it exposed to air. They didn't sew it up right away, in case there was an infection that might spread. The doctor came around the day before clean up and sew up time. After telling me what the procedure would be (which was a switch), I found out that his name was Dr. Hansen and that he was from someplace in northern Michigan. Sew up day was to be Thanksgiving Day, so I asked the doctor if I could have a local so that I could eat a true Thanksgiving meal.

Reference Note: Earlier I mentioned having trench foot. As you get into stage two, the feet get warm and hot and more painful. Walking around in the hospital, you could look at the made up beds and tell which guys had trench foot and which didn't. The normal method of making a bed in the hospital was to turn the top or head end down so that you would see about twelve to fourteen inches of the top white sheet. Trench foot patients had both ends of the bed turned back so that their feet stayed at room temperature even when they slept. To the best of my knowledge those with trench foot up to level three, or the gangrene/amputation stage, had only to stay off their feet as much as possible, and give their feet a little TLC, or tender loving care. If their feet were raw they may have been given an antiseptic cream. I do know that they did not wrap them. In my own case, by the time I left the general hospital, my feet were back to normal. My feet said, "Hey, I'm ready to go," while my mind said, "Feet … you go to hell."

As a side issue, when I was standing in that hospital hall waiting to board the ambulance to go to the general hospital, there were a lot of Japanese in GI uniforms coming in. I thought it was unusual. After I got out of the Army and saw the movie "Go for Broke," I realized who they were. They were the all-Japanese battalion who had volunteered for service, rather than remain in the detention center for Japanese civilians in California. Their first major action was to fight their way to an American battalion that had been surrounded and cut off. The Japanese suffered heavy casualties but attained their objective. They had to have been doing their thing at about the same time as we were running around getting trapped.

In addition to spending some of my life's happiest moments sleeping in a safe, dry warm bed, there was one other memory from the hospital that is worth recounting. My bed was positioned on one side of a doorway that lead into the large ward we were in. On the other side of the doorway was this big guy who had run into a machine gun. I was to find out later that he had played professional football. He was a very quiet man, which drew attention in its own way. He never engaged any of us in conversation or entered into comments being thrown back and forth, as was typical of any group of soldiers that are cooped up together. The fact that he never talked meant that he never complained, and that also was atypical.

The doctors had opened him up in several places. He had metal clamps about every inch and a half from near the top of his chest to well below his navel. You can only guess how they opened him up to remove and repair severed and damaged parts. He also had a colostomy. His right leg and his left arm were in casts. All of this, as I said, was the result of his having tangled with an enemy machine gun. One day they took him down to surgery. The method of transportation in the hospital, for non-ambulatory patients, was one guy on each end of a hand-carried litter. When they slid that guy from the bed onto the litter the two litter bearers darn near went to the floor. With extra effort and time they recovered enough to stand straight. It's hard to judge the size of a man lying in bed, and when you have to pick him up or carry him, proportions can be a bit of a shock. He was big and, I'm sure, solid.

When he came back from surgery he was still under anesthesia. They may not have had a recovery room at that hospital and if they did, I'm sure it was a short stay stop. As he was coming out of it he kept repeating, "They sewed up my arm, but they wouldn't sew up my goddamned side," over and over. What was behind that was the fact that his colostomy paraphernalia had to be cleaned at least daily, and it embarrassed him to have a female nurse do it. The evening orderly was a male and whenever "big man" could, he would defer it until the male orderly came on duty.

One day, to my surprise he asked me to give him a shave, which I did using a safety razor. While shaving him he talked long enough to tell me the head nurse was a "dumb bitch." (Hey, all right, this guy is human like the rest of us. He not only talks but also is capable of complaining. This was the kind of therapy he needed.) It seems that in giving him a shot a little blood oozed from the hypo prick. It didn't make any difference, as to the amount of blood or hurt he had experienced, but at least he was talking about it. I'll bet they dumped a pail of blood in that guy when they opened him up to connect all his innards together, and that was just to keep even with what must have been running out. I could picture the surgeon telling the nurse at the time, "Put a bigger tube on that transfusion supply, this guy is gaining on us."

Back to Platoon

While I was in the hospital, the breakthrough by the Germans occurred. The "Battle of the Bulge" was on. That meant emptying the hospitals out, posthaste. They practically removed the stitches from my wound on the way out of the hospital.

I arrived back at my platoon on December 24. Now isn't that nice? Back in time and on line for Christmas. When I got back there were two men from my original platoon. The platoon was on a stretched out defensive front. The new looie asked if I had done any patrol duty. Remembering the Army guideline about not volunteering, I gave him a quick, "No, sir." It worked—I didn't get sent out.

Things were uneventful and then on February 6, 1945, the division went on rest again, for eight days. We were mostly on the defense in our assigned sector. We saw some action, but nothing outstanding, so to speak. One day we took up positions occupying part of the French Maginot Line.

Reference Note: After WWI, the French erected a line of defense all along the border between France and Germany, just inside the French side. It was named the Maginot Line after the principal proponent of the idea, André Maginot, the French Minister of War at the time. The endeavor wound up being 12 to 16 miles deep and 940 miles long. The installations within the line included all types of antitank barricades, fortified observation posts, communication centers, infantry shelters, pillboxes, supply depots, etc. These structures had exterior walls that were a foot or more thick and reinforced with steel. Some of these home-like structures were called Block Houses, and there were four thousand of them scattered along the Maginot Line. Some structures above ground resembled different shapes of pillboxes, which I believe is how they got their name. The fortification pillboxes were not necessarily round and dome-shaped: some were cylindrical, some square, some rectangular (as were some of the pharmacists' pillboxes). Beneath the Maginot Line, the French built an elaborate cave network, including its own railroad. The cave/railroad network had many rooms for food storage, munitions, cafeterias, maintenance supplies, sleeping and resting quarters, and hospital necessities. Very elaborate, you might say. In WWII, the Germans simply went around the Belgian end of the line. Once they were behind the line, France fell in record time.

We were there for maybe two days and did not occupy the Maginot Line pillboxes or any of the rest of the Maginot Line proper, but dug our holes out in the open between the French defense structures. In addition to remembering that we didn't get to see the inside or underground of the Maginot Line, the other thing that sticks out is how we were relieved from our positions. The relief unit was a new division in combat. They moved in after dark via jeeps and trucks. We were on line, which meant that there was nothing between the enemy and us. These guys were driven up on line in trucks. The trucks were using the equivalent of parking lights to see where they were going. They were new to the line and out and out too damn noisy. We always tried to hold the noise down rather than give away our positions. These guys came in making more noise than a nervous pig stuck in a fence. Thank God the Germans didn't have any artillery near at hand, or their greetings on line would have been accompanied with some real fireworks—but not the kind they were used to as civilians. We said, "Give 'em time, they'll learn."

After we left, we heard that the Germans hit the new relief unit hard, before they had a chance to learn. Too bad! They were not the first new unit to catch hell their first time at bat. Earlier I mentioned escorting prisoners to the rear. The unit that we helped after the Germans broke through were also brand new in combat. The German intelligence was good at tracking divisions and I sometimes wonder if they didn't pick their moves so that they would test or try to break through the new ones in combat.

NEW LOOIE

Another place and time, we were dug in on a line that was shaped like a half circle. The ground in front of us was covered with waist-deep water, and extended for a good city block. The previous night a new looie had arrived. He mustered the platoon in the morning and told us that he had gone out the previous night to check, and that he didn't find anyone in the platoon awake on watch. He went on to say that he would continue checking up on us to make sure this didn't happen again.

We moved out and dug in just outside some town. All was quiet to our front, and we knew it (I don't know how, but we did). The new looie came out to check. It was very dark. One of the guys in my squad waited, aware of the sound of movement and the direction it was coming from. When the looie got close enough, the guy snapped the safety off of his M1 rifle. The looie heard the distinctive click and froze. My man purposely kept quiet. Finally, the looie spoke up, asking my man why he didn't challenge and ask for a password. My guy said he didn't know what was coming and wanted a better look. That looie never checked on us again. He turned out to be a real nice guy (not because of this incident, but just by his nature).

POTPOURRI

One time, we moved and relieved another division. It happened to be the 35th Division, which was brother Lynn's outfit. I asked for and received permission to try and find him. I was given 24 hours to do it in. I tried, but I could not locate him. Between having to hitchhike rides and having only twenty-four hours to look, it was pretty hopeless. It would have been real nice to have seen him there, with both of us fully arrayed in our uniforms of action, but it was not to be. The next time I was to see Lynn was at home. He got out of service ahead of me and was at home waiting for me, in his civvies, when I arrived.

House to House

I have already mentioned crossing the Rhine. There were no more major rivers to cross, so my division wasn't trying to establish any more beachheads.

Toward the end of the war we were in Germany, in the Ruhr valley. We did a lot of house-to-house cleanup work. The doors on most of the German houses were something else; extra thick with heavy, unyielding, latch mechanisms. It seemed to be law that they were locked at all times.

Picture going into a town where all the houses adjoin and run the length of the block. The fronts of the buildings sit three to four feet from the street, doorways flush with the face of the building. You run in the street, expecting to be shot at by some Kraut in hiding, trying to make it through the next door before it happens. You don't know what you're going to find in the house in front of you. You hit the door with your shoulder and it bounces you back. You kick it with your boot, nothing. You hit the panel of the door with the butt of your rifle—no dice. You try to shoot out the lock mechanism and it starts to give. You go in, never knowing if there is a Kraut waiting just inside the door with his safety off and his finger on the trigger. You have to check the main floor, cellar, and upstairs. It doesn't take long before your underfed butt is dragging.

If we went into a house and heard something in the basement, we would yell, "raus!" meaning "out!" or "come out!" A couple more yells and if there was no response, a grenade got thrown down. We didn't do this to every house, as we didn't carry enough grenades, but if we heard any kind of noise and there was no response, then it was grenade time. It would almost be suicide to walk down into a dark basement with a German that didn't want company.

If we drew fire from an adjoining building, we tried to pass from one house to the next via the adjoining wall, or try to find an opening of some kind between the two structures. The street was the danger area. When the houses weren't adjoining and we received some kind of fire from the house next to the one we were in, we would use a grenade launcher, firing through the window of one building into the window of the next, trying to drive out the enemy. Running through the streets, breaking down doors, running up and down stairs, pushing hard all the time, all the while maintaining a high state of alert was no fun.

POW Camp

We came to one town that we were not clearing house to house. We were on the far edge of town and high up. A block away, there was a good rise with a building on top. The looie told me to take a couple of men over there and check out the area.

When we got there, we were in a low area at the base of a hill. There was a cave that went under the hill, with an entranceway big enough to drive a truck through. I told the two guys that were with me to check it out, and I went to check the top of the hill. When I got up the hill, I could see an enclosure with barbed wire twelve feet high. I moved around to the front gate and looking through it, I could see many rows of barracks. I found that the gate was unlocked, so I went right on in. There were no guards that I could see. After a few minutes, someone stuck their head out of one of the barracks, saw me, and ducked back inside. A minute later, the same barrack door opened and people started steaming out. I realized that I was in a prisoner of war camp, and I was elated with the thought that I was their liberator. Soon, all of the prisoners started peeling out of their barracks. They hugged me and kissed me. Being kissed by men was not my speed, and their unshaven faces were much rougher than mine! There were women in the camp as well, and after looking at me closely, the expression on their faces seemed to say, "We are mighty grateful to be liberated, but kissing still has its limits." The men picked me up on their shoulders and carried me around.

After I was placed back on the ground, I reached in my jacket where I had a chunk of sausage. I had filched said sausage from a store that we had liberated earlier in the day. (It was a German store but we liberated it anyhow!) I held it out to the prisoners who were so eager to grab it that I purposely held onto it. It disappeared in no time, from my hand to theirs, dug out with their fingers.

None of the prisoners spoke English, so I used sign language to communicate with the "leaders." I managed to tell them to go back to their barracks and stay there until the Americans arrived, assuring them that when they arrived, they would be taken care of. The leaders got everyone to go back to their barracks. When I was left with only the four or five leaders, I pulled a bottle of wine from the inside of my jacket (same liberated store) and gave it to them. No bottle opener being handy, one of the guys whacked it on the corner of the building and broke the neck off. They wanted me to drink and I shook my head no, it was theirs. One guy held that broken neck over my mouth and began to pour. I swallowed as fast as I could, but it still ran down my front. That guy must have been a good whacker, as I didn't cough up any glass. They quickly downed the rest.

My two guys came back from checking out the cave, reporting that there was nothing there. One prisoner told us that there were a couple of German guards in a house one block away. We went to the house and I told my two buddies to go to the back and that I would go through the front. The POW was right, there were two German guards in the kitchen, sitting at a table eating as if the war was over. We helped their attitude become a reality: for them the war was now over. They offered no resistance; we searched them, liberating their personal belongings, and had them taken to the rear. To the victors go the spoils! That was the second POW camp my company relieved, and I got to go into this one first!

Wind Down

The war was starting to wind down, and we were just waiting for the official message that it was over. (The "official word" eventually came to us from our company commander, who called us all together to make the announcement.) My squad and I were billeted in a house, with our only real duty to act as military police and guard a semi-busy crossroads. There were two or three of us on duty at the crossroads at all times. Our main function was to interrogate all males that we thought were of military age. Those we considered of military age were herded to the "Rathaus," or city hall. There was a prison there, and if the German-speaking interrogator (an American) decided that the subject had been a soldier and had done a quick switch from military garb to civvies, then into the slammer he went.

Playing policeman at a crossroads was a little boring, really, but then one day things got a little more interesting. Halfway down the block from the crossroads was an underpass (above which ran railway tracks) which the Germans had completely closed off, except for a passenger-sized doorway on one end. They had dug two parallel rows of holes, three to four feet apart, cemented ten foot long railroad tracks in the holes, and then filled in the area between the rows with large stones and chunks of concrete. This effectively sealed the road off to all vehicle traffic larger than a bicycle.

The demolition group sized up the project, and laid cakes of dynamite at the base of each railroad track, tying each cake together with primer cord. They set the charged system off, and when the smoke cleared, the railroad tracks were laying on the ground in two well-organized rows, about five feet from where they had been cemented in. Those guys knew their art.

Earlier on in the war, we had come across many places where the Germans had cut the trees along the road, leaving them lying across the road to stop any vehicle traffic, at least temporarily. This tactic was mostly used in wooded areas, especially if the road had a bank on either side. Without banks, mobile units would simply go off the road and around the blockage. The

Germans would sometimes use dynamite to fell the trees, and at times we would come across a section of trees with unexploded dynamite still strapped to them. Most likely, they had moved out too fast and left the job unfinished. Sometimes they would position antitank guns just beyond the roadblock, and give anyone who tried to get through a hard time. This would be a time to move the infantry forward and put them into action.

Zombie

I used the word "zombie" earlier and I would like to clarify what I mean. According to my terminology, a zombie is someone showing an early degree of combat fatigue. Since the infantry suffered more cases of combat fatigue than any other branch of the Army (with possible exception of the Air Force), I would like to give it more than a few words. Read on and I'll tell you about it.

COMBAT FATIGUE

When John Glenn returned from his second trip in space, he said, "It gave me a high to see planet Earth from space, but the time the adrenalin really flowed was when I was in combat." What causes adrenalin to flow? When a person gets very excited or frightened, the adrenal gland secretes a hormone called adrenalin. Adrenalin makes the heart beat faster, causing higher blood flow, which results in more oxygen being taken to the brain and other parts of the body. It also increases blood sugar level. In this heightened state, the body and brain are now better equipped to deal with the sudden emergency. (Incidentally, if the emergency passes quickly and the body doesn't require the rush of blood sugar, the body responds by causing the person to have severe trembling, also known as "the shakes." Having the shakes uses up the extra energy not required by the emergency.)

If you are subjected to near death experiences, months on end, does the body still pump adrenalin? I don't know. I can't say that I was aware of the effects of it happening at the time. What I can attest to though, is what I believe happens to the mind and psyche over time while in combat.

To review, the average combat infantryman eats near starvation-sized rations, sleeps in holes, endures any type of weather wearing whatever is on his back, is constantly on the move, pulls fifty percent guard at night, and doesn't know if he will survive the day or the week. He gets run down, his physical state influencing his mental state or his mind. The mind is also eaten away by direct enemy fire, tank fire, ordinary artillery fire, mortar, machine gun, rifle fire, and land mines, in that order. Over time, these things nibble away at the mind, along with near death experiences, and seeing death and the dead. All of this has a cumulative effect. If the bad things experienced and the rate of occurrence is fast, then the mind recovers even less. Personally, I didn't look at our own dead in an attempt to avoid some of this. Seeing a dead German didn't bother me nearly as much as seeing an American dead.

The mind has its limit or breaking point, which varies from one individual to the next. When that point is reached, the mind starts taking its own course of defensive action. This action can take many routes. Perhaps I can define "breaking point" as the point when rational thinking starts absenting itself or in the severe case, leaves completely. The severest case is when the mind shuts down completely, closes out the outside world and the person is in a walking coma. Again, the mind is protecting itself.

The environment the subject was raised in, during his or her formative years, mostly forms that crossover line and its level. You might call it the mind tolerance level. The other major influence that establishes the mind's tolerance level is indoctrination. All infantry training has some form of indoctrination. Understandably, as part of its defensive measures, the Army indoctrinated and helped tune the mind for its possible coming abuses. The whole civilian population is indoctrinated during wartime. We have come to know this as propaganda.

The mind's tipping point was challenged most in the Air Force, more so than the infantry. This was because the personnel flying in combat, in the bombers, had such limited options of defense or recourse of any kind while in the thick of things. They knew the threat to their lives was coming, they knew the forms of that threat, and they had to just sit there and ride it out, hoping that they had the luck to live through it this time. With antiaircraft bursting all around them, there was nothing to do but sit, hope, pray, and wait to be wounded or killed. There was no place to run to and it did no good to play dead. Having no choices and no control really took its toll on the mind.

The zombie stage was the early stage of combat fatigue. In this stage, you appear to be staring without seeing, walking like you are on remote control, with slow responses, as though the mind is somewhere else and has a near total lack of interest. You are showing signs of deep mental fatigue and, with infantrymen, physical fatigue as well.

In the next stage, you start babbling, can't tell which direction sounds are coming from, can't differentiate, and can't reason.

In the worst stage, the mind shuts itself off to the outside world. The body is there and can function, but the mind's only output is the auto-mechanical functions. The person is in a state of unconsciousness, blackout, or coma.

Getting wounded gave me enough rest, physically and mentally, to allow my systems to back off. Some of the fatigue of nerves and fears of the mind were deep and would take time.

After I returned from service, when falling asleep at night, I had to account for every little noise I heard. Nightmares, when they did occur, were more intense than usual. With nerves on edge, I was still like a caged animal on the inside. On the outside,

I know I appeared quite normal. As I said earlier, for many years, I would get worked up inside when I talked about being in combat.

The saying is "time heals all wounds." Thankfully, it can also heal the mind's wounds. Today, I can not only talk about being in combat, but also overtalk about it (as you may have observed). I do enjoy telling others what it was like, although I feel that my words of description are inadequate in drawing a true picture. What I can say, though, is "I have tried."

When I talk to another who has been "there," it is totally different. It's like a good one-on-one conversation with a long absent brother or sister. It warms the body and mind, or maybe I should say "spirit."

IN HINDSIGHT

In general, the German soldiers were good soldiers, and they fought well. Toward the end of the war, the Germans conscripted older men and teenagers, thirteen years of age and up, and their fighting quality wasn't as good. It was demoralizing seeing the young dead. When the young German soldiers surrendered, they were usually crying. They were probably indoctrinated with the idea that if they surrendered they would be shot.

There was a group who were called Hitler's Youth. They were well trained and in defensive positions did a good job.

If I had a fault with my behavior during the war, I would say it was in not hating enough. At the same time, had I harbored intense hatred, it may have produced a different outcome for me. I mentioned earlier that I did hate the SS and snipers. Who knows?

The day of the war that I have Monday morning quarterbacked, rerun through my mind, and mentally relived the most has been "Wipeout Day" or November 18, 1944. Oh, the many times I have thought of what I could have done differently that day. Usually, my rational mind kicks in after a bit and I tell myself that no matter how much or how long I think about it, I will never be able to change a single event of that day, nor the lay of a single blade of grass in that field. Only time will tell if I am to remember it the longest, but I am betting against that. WWII was big and long.

My division was an attack division and its record proves it was effective in crossing rivers and establishing bridgeheads. Doing that kind of work, the casualties are high. Records state that the Division took 27,659 prisoners. During a month and a half, prior to and overlapping the war's end, we set up roadblocks (which I mentioned earlier) and interrogated every male of military age. They were all dressed in civilian clothes. These men were taken to staging areas. This action accounted for an additional 7,807 prisoners.

The 79th Division's casualty listing was 2,476 killed in action and an additional 467 died later of wounds, also 10,971 wounded in action and 1,699 captured or missing in action.

After the war's end, including the war in the Pacific, we were shuffled around, based on how many points each person had. Points were accredited based on total time in service, time spent overseas, so much for each battle star, so much for each meritorious medal, and so much for each Purple Heart. Those with the highest points total were rotated home to the States first.

After shifting around through several different camps, my outfit wound up at a camp that had a German prisoner of war enclosure within its boundaries. As part of our duties, we had to guard this enclosure. It was surrounded by the regular high barbed wire fence, with guard towers higher up, and rows of barracks inside. When it was my turn at guard, I was placed in charge of posting the detail and then standing watch at the booth at the main gate. With the shuffling of troops going on, a bunch of medics or hospital personnel had moved in with us. They had to stand guard, too, and these guys had never fired a rifle! They were issued M1s for this. When it came time to position the guards, I went up in the tower with each man, loaded the rifle, put the safety in the off position, and stood it in the corner. I told them not to touch that damn gun unless they saw a prisoner trying to go through the wire fence ... and should that happen, point the rifle as best they could and pull the trigger a few times. When their shift was over, I went back to each tower, unloaded their rifles, pocketed the ammo, and marched the medics back to their quarters. If those prisoners had any intention of leaving, this would have been the time to make a break. My guess was that none of the prisoners wanted to leave. Where would they go? If they remained prisoners, their eventual exit would be legal and documented.

It was around this time that I got a leave and went to England and spent a week with Ed. I slept in his barracks, ate in his mess hall, and went out with him and his buddy, Joe Connolly, from Boston. I didn't stand a chance keeping up with their pub capacities. I could keep up on the way to the pub, but not after. I was with a couple of seasoned veterans of another sort.

Rebellious

When I returned to my unit, I was at least two days late. It wasn't that I had overstayed my leave, but because of the train schedule coming back from England. I reported back, as military procedure dictated, to the Company Commander, Lieutenant Cooch III, West Point graduate. I didn't know what would come down. I walked into his office, stood in front of his desk, came to attention, saluted, and said, "Sergeant McDonnell reporting back as ordered, sir." He looked at me and said, "I think you need a bath. Go take one." I said, "Yes, sir," saluted, did an about face and exited. He was a good man indeed!

I had one other personal dealing with the Company Commander. When we first got to the quarters we were in, I was a little rebellious in mind and manner. I skipped all formations and stayed in bed in the morning. I got up just in time to be last in line for breakfast. The Company First Sergeant told me that I should fall out at the required times with the rest. I said "sure," and didn't. My thoughts were that all this jazz was useless; after all, the job was over. It wasn't many days after that when another sergeant came to me and said "I have a message for you. The Company Commander, Lieutenant Cooch III, has requested your presence along with the rest of the Company, at retreat formation this evening." There's no need to discuss how that came out. That lieutenant had been in combat with us and as I said before, he was a good man. Who was I to turn down such a personal request and so politely stated?

Well, there are a lot of other little stories I have skipped over, but I think this has been long enough. I might mention one thing that sticks out in my memory, having to do with bringing things to an end in Europe, and that was the handing in of our rifles. It was a joy to no longer have to carry it, but a feeling of being defenseless set in. I can understand why in Western movies, the cowboys said they felt naked when they removed their gun.

By now you should have a good general gist and feeling as to what the life and trials of a dogface were like in WWII.

Mustered Out

I was mustered out of the Army on January 4, 1946 at Camp Atterbury, Indiana. This day, too, brought on a feeling of mixed emotions. The feeling that I was out and no longer had to live exactly as the Army dictated was offset with the feeling that I was on my own and had to provide and take care of myself. I shrugged the lonely thoughts off and headed for the train station. Brother Lynn was already home, and Allen and Ed were coming to join us soon. As I recall there were no parties held as such, but we did do some drinking upon the return of each brother. Legally, I couldn't buy a drink in a bar, as I was not yet twenty-one, but I could if I was in uniform. So, guess what? On weekends when I went out with a friend to an "establishment," back on came the uniform.

All of us were happy to be home again, and thankful for having survived our duties. Happiness was a family reunited, together again! I do believe that we had a sense of pride, each of us in our own way, in having been there, although we never addressed the issue of pride in what we had done, ever. We told each other interesting stories of things said and done in service and never bypassed a story that was humorous. We had taken a large step in living and experiencing new horizons, which in hindsight brought about seismic changes in our lives. Now we had to get to know each other again. We could do that. Time was on our side.

DECORATIONS

ROBERT McDONNELL

Sgt. a.s.n. 36877952

Combat Infantry Badge

European Theater of Operations

Ribbon with 4 stars [1]

Purple Heart

Presidential Unit Citation

Good Conduct Ribbon [2]

American Theater of Operations Ribbon

Three Hash Bars or Gold Stripes/Worn on left sleeve [3]

WWII Victory Medal

Bronze Star Medal

[1] One star for each major campaign. There were four major campaigns in Europe that the 79th Division participated in.

[2] These ribbons meant nothing as they were near automatic.

[3] One stripe for each six months overseas.

In addition, my Regiment received two French Croix de Guerre citations, one with embroidered Palm Streamer, PARROY FOREST, and the second with embroidered Palm Streamer, NORMANDY TO PARIS. ("Croix de Guerre" is French for "Cross of War".)

Reference note: In Army talk, "Hash Bar" = "Hershey Bar," "All Medals and Ribbons" = "Fruit Salad."

Reference note: On February 4, 1944 President Roosevelt authorized the award of a Bronze Star Medal for heroic or meritorious action, for personnel while engaged against the enemy in combat. The decree also made the issuance of the award retroactive to the beginning of WWII. The idea was that if an individual did something outstanding, it was to be recognized with an award, i.e., a Bronze Star Medal.

After a study by the government, conducted in 1947, authorization was made to award the Bronze Star Medal to any soldier who had received the Combat Infantry Badge or Combat Medical Badge during WWII.

We now have Bronze Star Medals that have been issued under two different sets of decrees. The Medals are not different, only the conditions for having received one: those issued during WWII for heroic or meritorious action and those issued to all who had a Combat Infantry Badge or Combat Medical Badge. Brother Lynn receive his for some heroic or outstanding action, and I got mine by a retroactive decree two years after the war had ended. Truth be known!

SQUAD PICTURES

Below are pictures of the guys that were in my squad when the war ended. I have no idea where the camera or the film came from. Upon studying the pictures, I realized they were taken with more than one camera. We were billeted in a civilian apartment building in Witten, Germany. It was here that we got to throw off the dust and dirt of living in fields and sleeping on or in the ground or on a floor. We started putting military creases in our clothes and looking civilized. Once again I don't remember where the clothes iron came from, or the ironing board, for that matter. It was nice to stay clean again!

Figure 2. Left: James C. Cave; Right: Odie G. Claxton

These two guys came in together as replacements. How long they were in combat with us I can't remember, but what I do remember was that they were flown over from the States, and having joined us together, they buddied up with each other and always hung together.

When the war officially ended, we were billeted in a house and we took up wrestling as a form of exercise. Cave was very fast with his moves and Claxton, having had formal wrestling in high school, was a little perplexed with non-formal wrestling. They were both eighteen years old.

Figure 3. Left: William (Big Stoop) Doyle; Right: Jack Odum

I was the one that hung the nickname "Big Stoop" on Doyle. He reminded me of a character in a comic strip that I read when I was in grade school. He never seemed to mind the nickname much until after the war, when we were stationed in Czechoslovakia. We were in formation one day and the lieutenant gave the order, "Dress right, dress." As a result of this order, all troops will be aligned shoulder to shoulder, one arms length apart and in a straight line. The lieutenant then stands on the end of the line and sights down it to see if all of the men are in a straight line. Having done so, the lieutenant said, "Big Stoop, pull in your belly." For some reason Doyle didn't like being called Big Stoop in that situation.

Doyle was from a farm in Ohio, about six feet three or four, and loose and gangly to the point of looking awkward. I say he looked awkward, but he wasn't. One time while standing in line, he and Fleming were horsing around. Doyle took a step back from Fleming and with his right foot kicked Fleming's helmet liner off, quick and clean. Fleming was a lot surprised and a little stunned. It is something else to meditate on afterwards that a size twelve (or larger) Army boot went past the end of your nose only far enough away to pick up the front tip of the helmet liner, which projected no more than two inches from your forehead.

When we first moved to Czechoslovakia, Doyle was pissed at me for something. When I asked why, he told me I had told one of the other guys in the squad to do something and when that guy hadn't, I told him, Doyle, to do it. That's a big no-no in the Army. I probably apologized, but it was not all over.

They set up a boxing ring to, once again, keep the troops in shape and we had an experienced amateur boxer as an instructor. One guy, who knew about Doyle's feelings toward me, suggested Doyle and I get in the ring together. I couldn't refuse so I told myself, "What the hell, a lot of people have been knocked out and they didn't die." Really, the gloves we wore were so big and stuffy it would be a fluke if someone got knocked out. You could swing with enough force to drive someone across the ring, which he did, but a knockout, no. We each got in a few good licks and with no real harm done we de-ringed feeling better toward each other.

Odum was kind of a quiet man in combat, doing what had to be done with no fuss about it. He was a few years older than I, and was the only man in the squad that was with the division when the division landed on the shores of Normandy. He had been wounded twice and had two Purple Hearts to attest to same.

Franklin: I can't remember if his name was Ray Franklin or Franklin Ray. He was a farmer and a hard man to get along with, as he didn't like taking an order, especially from someone younger than himself.

Figure 4. Left: Franklin, Romine, Santiago, and Fleming (crouching); Right: Santiago and Robinson

Romine: I can't remember his first name, but I do remember that he was very strong. When we wrestled within the squad, he would maneuver his opponent around until he got both arms under him. Romine would then get both of his feet and legs under himself and lift his adversary up and up until his rival was completely over Romine's head. He would then say, "Give up?" The answer was always "yes." If I were to guess, I would say his first name was Vincent.

Domingo Santiago: If my memory is right, he was around, in combat that is, quite a while. He was from New York, New York, and worked as an assistant chef in civilian life. I know he had been wounded as least once, so he had an interruption in his on line time. He was always early to rise in combat, regardless of whether it was his turn to stand guard duty or not. The first thing he did in the morning was make a fire in his hole, eat, then give his rifle a going over to clean it. He probably had the cleanest rifle in the company, if not the whole damn regiment.

Fleming: He is the one that "Big Stoop" Doyle kicked the hat off of. After the war's end, Fleming, Lynton (the squad leader), and I hung around a bit together. One day, Fleming borrowed the "grease gun" that I had been carrying as a weapon. At this time, every man still carried a weapon of some kind. We were going to go out together that evening. He returned my grease gun as he had borrowed a .45 and its accompanying holster from someone else. He and I were standing out on the sidewalk waiting for Lynton. Earlier when he returned my grease gun, he told me he had fired it and laughingly told me I would probably have to clean it . While we were standing on the sidewalk, I asked him if there was a round of ammunition in the chamber of his .45. He said no without paying attention to me. I was standing to his rear and I reached down and opened the flap of holster, exposing the handle and trigger assembly of the .45. Taking hold of the .45 and pointing it away from his leg, I pulled the trigger. I blew the end of his holster out and startled him as the gun went off. Being a little irate, he said, "What in hell did you do that for?" I said, "You told me there wasn't a round in the chamber and now you can clean that gun and I'll clean my grease gun." What goes a round comes a round!

Myron Robinson: He was the squad elder and I don't remember his true age at that time. He must have been in his late thirties, and was prematurely balding. He hailed from New York and we called him "Pops." He, too, had been wounded earlier and had at least one Purple Heart. He was quiet, likeable, and intelligent.

Harry was our squad leader. He hailed from Pontiac, Michigan. We made friends during the war and hung around together

Figure 5. Left: Harry Lynton; Right: Me

after hostilities had ceased. We were separated when they started moving everyone around according to the number of points
each had (which determined their position on the to-be-shipped-
home list). He was the son of a baker and as such, knew a little
something about baking. One time toward the end of hostilities,
we were in a small village. He said, "These are the ingredients
I need, and if we scout around we may be able to make a couple
of pies." We did and he did. I don't recall what the filling was but
I'm sure we ate every crumb.

I visited Harry after the war and by this time, he was married
and they were living in a new home that was not quite complete.
For whatever reason, the camaraderie was no longer there. Life
and times move on.

The picture of me was taken at the same time as the rest of the squad pictures were taken.

Figure 6. Sailing home

This picture was taken on the boat on the way home. We disembarked from the port of Le Havre, France, which is on the Mediterranean Sea. It was in December, and after we were on the Atlantic Ocean for a while, we ran into a storm. The boat listed to the point that we exceeded the critical return angle. If the angle of no return was, say, forty-three degrees, we went a few degrees past that. We were told that our adventures in the troop carrier had been printed in a French newspaper. At the height of the storm, we remained in our bunks, five high and just enough room to roll into the bunks. As the ship pitched and rolled, we, while lying flat, spread our legs apart to the width of the bunk for balance, while at the same time holding on to the sides of the bunk for fear of being dumped out onto the floor. We could not sit up in the bunks as there wasn't enough room, and you can imagine the floor as being slippery from you know what. What a sad ending it might have been for so many to have been lost at sea after all of our previous escapades.

Before I finish here, I would like to share a little story about one of the guys I ran into just before we loaded onto the boat for our ride back home to the States. As I mentioned before, the troops were from everywhere, as they were amassed together based on the Army's priority listing. On the train that took us to Le Havre (actually it was a boxcar full of GIs, as opposed to a passenger car), one of the guys in the car, new to me, was a real sad sack. (A sad sack in Army slang is a guy that never seems to get anything right, either as part of his character or maybe intentionally.) This guy's clothes looked like he had slept in them from the time he had joined the Army, his hair was never combed and his hat sat on his head but was never placed there. On top of everything else, he never tied his shoes.

I don't know how long we were on or in that boxcar but it was several days, and it was definitely low priority, as we made more stops than a dog in a telephone pole yard.

Now for the good part of Sad Sack: every time we stopped, he would either convince some civilian to get him food or he hopped off the train and scrounged around and brought something back. He always got back on time to be on the train without it leaving him, even if it was close sometimes. In the boxcar, he would be cooking eggs and eating homemade bread while we, jealously looking on, ate our K-rations.

At the staging area in Le Havre, the lines of barracks were headed up with a mess hall on the ends. Once again, I don't know how long we were there, but I noticed Sad Sack had apples and oranges to spare. I asked him in a friendly voice, "How do you manage to come up with all that?" He told me he just goes down the line, into and out of each mess hall, taking only the fruit they have to offer. I told him tomorrow you take me along. He did, and we moved out of our area completely and went in this mess hall. Lo and behold, when we got inside, all the help were Afro-American. We proceeded through the line toward where the fruit was, which was at the end of the line, when one of the staff asked us where we had come from, we being white and all that. We told him we were from a new unit that had just arrived and there would be a whole group following us. Their only thought was they were only used to serving their own and here comes a new group they hadn't planned on. We moved out with our fruit and that was the last foraging for me. I was satisfied from then on to play it by the book.

I was always prone to getting seasick and the ship we left on proved no exception. Twenty minutes after casting off from the dock, I was in the bathroom tossing my cookies (or was it apples?). The trip home was worth it, though.

I recall, too, that on the train (passenger cars this time) that hauled us from the landing docks to our new Army camp, there was a little treat for us. One of the guys had a portable radio that I have no idea from whence it came. He tuned in to "The Lone Ranger." We all listened intently and as I said, it was a real treat.

When we arrived at the camp, our first meal was steak, milk, and ice cream plus all the trimmings. Later on, I called home to announce my arrival. I think I talked for ten minutes and it cost over eleven dollars. Funny, the things we remember!

Figure 7. Left: Cave; Right: Cave, Santiago, and Robinson

Cave not only stopped to smell the flowers, he sat and decided to stay awhile.

Figure 8. Fleming and jeep

I don't know where the jeep came from, nor who it belonged to. For sure, it didn't belong to anyone in our Company, as all of us were infantry. I don't think Fleming stole it, but if someone told me he had, I wouldn't have hesitated to believe that person.

Figure 9. Lynton and I

There's that jeep again.

Lynton wasn't crocked in this picture but it wasn't beyond him to imbibe, and if he heard me saying this he would say, "You're damned right." One time, after we had left this area of Witten, we went to this town together as there was some kind of a bash going on. The establishment was selling Schnapps (liquor made from potatoes), wine, and beer. Neither of us had any money, so we decided to go around and bum drinks from anyone and at any table. They didn't shoo us away as we were both sergeants and they don't usually go around glad-handing and sharing your table drinks. We wound up drinking a real duke's mixture and got really sloshed. Lynton was supposed to be in charge of a guard detail that night, but there were no repercussions from his absence. You might say he was bucking to become a private that night. Whatever!

Figure 10. Left: "Mack" Wilson and me; Right: "The Good, the Bad, and the Ugly."

"Mack" Wilson was our platoon guide. He joined us late, actual "war time," so I didn't really get to know him. This picture doesn't do him justice, as it makes him look like he's blind and a little shell-shocked.

The picture of me with the machine gun was taken just as the war was ending. I did not carry the Thompson machine gun as a weapon, I only posed with it.

Figure 11. Jack Odum

This picture was also taken just as the war was ending. I don't know where the horse came from, but I do know Odum is the one with the helmet on.

Figure 12. German hound. (P.S. You can figure out which is which.)

Another picture taken as the war was ending. The dog I am holding is not the dog that I offered the C-ration to, as was mentioned earlier. The dog in this picture looks like he would be full if he licked one of our empty ration cans: and when we emptied a food can, the only thing left was scrape marks!

RETURN TRIPS

My wife and I made several trips to France, once just before retiring from GM (in 1982), and once again after retiring (in 1994). The second trip coincided with the fiftieth anniversary of the invasion of Normandy.

On the trip in 1982, we were accompanied by my wife's two sisters and their husbands, and since my brother is married to my wife's oldest sister, I can say that we were accompanied by my wife's two sisters, my brother, and brother-in-law. The brother-in-law was Réal Seguin and his wife Thérèse, and my brother is Ed and his wife Cécile.

On the first trip, starting up in Normandy, we motored along some of the route that I had walked back in '44 / '45. When we came to La Haye-du-Puits, I of course called for a picture stop. We then continued on, and generally speaking, visited Biarritz in the south for about four days, and then headed north, with, of all places in mind, wouldn't you know it, Charmes, France. There were things about Charmes that made it one of the most outstanding places on my original rifle toting excursion. Maybe it was because it was there that I got to lord it over Joe Lopez, lying there so comfortably. Maybe it was because we took the high ground, with its beautiful sights overlooking the city and countryside. Maybe it was the type of action that went on as we closed in on our objective. Maybe it was the monument that we erroneously thought had been erected in honor of our division in WWII. More probably it was the type of action that had had so many facets that I could relate to, as opposed to fighting for some village or town that was half flattened, with rubble everywhere but nothing distinctive about it. I do know, too, that I had a sense of pride at being at the top of that hill and having "taken" that place. The following pictures will give you a chance to see and share what I often simply referred to as the "Monument."

The second trip was twelve years later, and my wife and I stayed at a home outside of Paris. The couple that owned it, along with their two children, had resided in Saginaw for two years. Their names were Jean and Brigitte Botti. When the older of the two daughters entered school here, she knew no English. My wife, being fluent in French and having taught both English and French, was asked to tutor her in English, and since the mother and the preschool-aged youngest daughter were in the same boat, language-wise, the women started to become good friends. As time passed, we all became good friends.

While visiting their place in France, we were contacted by Mike Cousin and his wife Monique. Mike said he had some business in Strasbourg, France, and asked if my wife and I would like to accompany them. We said, "certainement" ("certainly" or "surely" in English). We stopped overnight on our way there, and you will never guess the name of the town—you guessed it: Charmes!

Pictured in Figure 13, from left to right: my wife Marge, Thérèse Seguin, my brother Ed, his wife Cécile, and Réal Seguin. Brother Ed and I could speak only a few words in French, but the other four spoke French fluently, so we had no barriers as to communicating, wherever we went.

Figure 13. The six of us that toured France in 1982.

Figure 14. Entering the city of Charmes, 1982.

Figure 15. It's hard to make out the Cross of Lorraine that is on the face of the obelisk. The man closest to the camera is my brother-in-law Réal, with brother Ed at the table on the monument, and one of the wives at the end and leaning over the edge.

Figure 16. Yours truly, looking down the hill in front of the monument.

Figure 17. Looking down the hill. The trees and the brush in the center were not there in 1944.

Figure 18. My wife and I at the "monument" table, 1982.

Figure 19. Bullet-scarred rail, from the German machine gunner at the base of the hill.

Figure 20. Mike Cousin and me, at the monument, 1994.

Encore tous mes remerciements et bien cordialement [signature]

L'EST RÉPUBLICAIN

NANCY-HOUDEMONT 54185 HEILLECOURT Cedex

NOM *SERRIÈRE* Prénom *Richel*

Correspondant à *CHARMES* Le *11. 9. 94*
88130 AVRAINVILLE

DIMANCHE
11 septembre 1994

L'EST RÉPUBLICAIN

VOSGES

N° 35041

7,00 F

FONDÉ EN 1889
CPP 65 244

De la Belgique
à la Suisse

Un GI nommé Robert Mc Donnell

Il y a 50 ans, il était l'un des premiers soldats américains à fouler le sol carpinien pour le libérer. Emotion du souvenir.

« Revoir depuis ma chambre d'hôtel ce monument de Lorraine, si plein de souvenirs et découvert il y a 50 ans dans des conditions dramatiques et pourtant avec l'exaltante énergie d'un jeune libérateur du sol français, m'a empli d'une immense fierté et d'un vrai bonheur. Aussitôt il a fallu que je m'y rende ». A la tête de douze hommes d'un commando du 314e régiment de la 79e Division d'Infanterie américaine, Robert Mc Donnell fut l'un des premiers libérateurs de la ville.

Débarqué en Normandie quelques jours après le fameux jour J et malgré de difficiles combats sur la France traversée, l'homme garde particulièrement les événements de Charmes dans sa mémoire et dans son cœur.

Pour Preuve, sa commémoration à lui ne pouvait être qu'au pays de Barrès.

Notre croix de Lorraine

Deux jours durant, au mois de juin de cette année, l'ex cadre de la General-Motors aujourd'hui retraité, accompagné de son épouse et d'amis français a revécu ces heures de septembre 1944. « Notre commando devait supprimer les forces allemandes installées comme des chiens de garde au monument de Lorraine. Il nous a fallu les surprendre en contournant la colline avec des ruses de Sioux par le flanc ouest. Une stratégie qui nous a permis, après de rudes combats, de venir à bout de cette résistance et d'ouvrir la route aux armées de la libération ».

Parmi les souvenirs les plus marquants racontés par notre Américain, la Croix de Lorraine reste encore son étonnement. « Notre régiment portait depuis toujours

un béret avec la croix de Lorraine et quel ne fut pas notre étonnement de découvrir cette immense Croix de Lorraine sur cette colline conquise. Ce ne pouvait être en notre honneur ».

Lance-grenade

Une autre péripétie apporte également le sourire sur le visage de Robert Mc Donnell qui se souvient avoir découvert pour la première fois des fusils lance-grenades abandonnés par les Allemands en fuite. Curieux de les utiliser il visa un petit boqueteau duquel s'enfuient, à sa grande surprise, plusieurs Allemands effrayés.

Et sans cesse, l'homme s'est remémoré toute ces pages vécues dans notre pays. Elles restent en lui comme autant de petites marques indélébiles entourées du célèbre « J'avais vingt ans ».

Un retour ému pour Robert Mc Donnell.

Aujourd'hui l'ancien GI des années 44-45, les yeux emplis d'émotion, s'en est retourné vers sa ville de Detroit. Parmi la reconnaissance des Carpiniens pour ses libérateurs, célébrée aujourd'hui, nul doute que Robert Mc Donnell sentira une petite brise Vosgienne souffler sur ses souvenirs.

Figure 21. Article in *L'Est Républicain*

FRENCH NEWSPAPER ARTICLE

In addition to seeing the monument and the village, I asked the hotel clerk if there was a news reporter in the town. After answering in the affirmative, he told me he would ask the reporter to come to the hotel and listen to my story. Bear in mind that although the fiftieth anniversary of the invasion was still being celebrated, the actual liberation of Charmes didn't take place until mid-September of 1944. I told the reporter the sequence of events that I experienced as the city was being liberated and asked that if my narrative appeared in print, would he send me a copy? He assured me he would. Here is a copy of said article (which appeared on September 11, 1994) along with my apology for it not having better survived the photocopying process. Marguerite, my wife, did the translation and stuck to a literal translation as opposed to a loose one.

Translation

The headline: "A GI named Robert McDonnell." The subheading: "Fifty years ago, he was one of the first American soldiers to trample the French grounds to free it."

Emotion of the Memory

"To see from my hotel room the Monument of Lorraine, so full of memories and discovered 50 years ago in dramatic conditions, yet with exalting energy of a young liberator of French soil, filled me with immense pride and true happiness. I had to get there immediately." At the head of 12 men of a commando of the 314th regiment of the 79th division of the American Infantry, Robert McDonnell was one of the first liberators of the city.

Having landed in Normandy, a few days after the famous D-Day and in spite of the difficult battles while crossing France, the man keeps in his heart and memories, the events that took place in Charmes. To prove this, his commemoration could only be of the nation of Barres. [The area in and around Charmes stood out and remained clear in my memory.]

Our Cross of Lorraine

For two days, in June of this year [1994], the ex-General Motors employee, nowadays retired, accompanied by his wife and a French friend and his spouse, relived the hours of September 1944. Our commando was to suppress the German forces situated like dogs guarding the Monument of Lorraine. We, the GI's surprised them by using wise tactics around the west side of the hill. A strategy that allowed us to offer resistance and to clear the way for the liberation Army.

"Among the memories recounted by our American soldier, the Cross of Lorraine is the most outstanding. Our regiment [division] had always worn a beret bearing the insignia of the cross of Lorraine [We wore the patch bearing the insignia of the Cross of Lorraine on our shoulder in reality, but his idea of it being on a beret is more romantic.] and imagine what it was to discover this immense Cross of Lorraine on the conquered hill. We assumed it was to honor us [or to honor what our division had done in WWI]."

Grenade Launcher

Another adventure brings a smile to Robert McDonnell's face as he remembers having discovered a grenade launcher and gun abandoned by the fleeing Germans. Curious to utilize them, he aimed at a bush and to his great surprise, several German soldiers, in hiding, ran away.

One memory after another, the American man relived all these pages of history experienced in our country. Those memories for him are like indelible marks surrounded with his famous saying: "I was twenty years old." [I was nineteen all the time that I was in combat.] Today, the former GI of 1944-1945, filled with emotion, returned to his home by way of Detroit, MI. Besides the gratitude for its liberator felt today, there is no doubt that Robert McDonnell will also feel a soft breeze from the Vosges [mountainous area] blowing on his souvenirs [memories].

Merci beaucoup, Monsieur Mike Serrierre. [Thank you very much, Mike Serriere. Mike didn't speak English, so Mike Cousin translated my story during the interview.] Truth be known, I did not lead 12 commandos, but was one of a rifle platoon comprised of about 40 men. Things do sometimes get lost, or gained, in the translation. I'm not complaining, mind you.

ADDENDUM

The 79th Division published its own newspaper during WWII and I have one copy of that paper. The paper is dated June 19, 1945 and is Volume 1 No. 1. The date establishes the fact that it was printed after the war had ended. The paper is one large page, folded and printed on both sides, making it four pages long. The name of the newspaper is, strangely enough, LORRAINE CROSS. The following are verbatim excerpts:

NORMANDY TO CZECHOSLOVAKIA:

2800-MILE DASH ACROSS FRANCE AND GERMANY FEATURES 79TH'S CRACK COMBAT RECORD IN ETO

Three years ago this month the 79th Infantry Division was reactivated at Camp Pickett, Va. One year ago today it was committed to its first combat in World War II, in the Normandy hedgerow country southwest of Valognes. In ten months of hard fighting it has compiled one of the finest combat records in the ETO. In this record are three outstanding "firsts": First into Cherbourg, first across the Seine, first American division to stand on the Rhine. Few divisions have served under as many Higher Headquarters: All three Army Groups, four of the five U.S. armies, nine of the sixteen U.S. corps.

The Division's combat itinerary — approximately 2800 miles — is one of the longest. Predominantly a spearhead and "river crossing" unit, it featured in nearly all the important Allied campaigns in the West: The seizure of Cherbourg, the great breakthrough and the closing of the Argentan-Falaise Pocket, the dash to the Seine and then on to Belgium, the drive into Lorraine, the piercing of the Vosges and the clearing of Alsace, the containing of the enemy's desperate Alsatian counteroffensive, the clearing of the Rhineland, crossing of the Ruhr and reduction of the Ruhr pocket. In prisoners alone the Division has accounted for the equivalent of three enemy divisions. Enemy casualties in killed and wounded are reckoned as many times greater.

This was the record that prompted Ninth U.S. Army to select the 79th as one of its two assault units in the Rhine River crossing. Here, in intentionally cold fact and a minimum of color is that record in detail:

On June 12, 1944, the 79th's first elements reached Utah Beach and during the following week the remainder of the Division assembled near Ste. Mere Eglise in VII Corps reserve. It was this week that saw the cutting of the Cherbourg Peninsula and the unleashing of First Army's drive to capture the great port at its tip. The importance of taking Cherbourg at once was underlined by a spell of rough weather at the beaches which made imperative the Allied possession of a good harbor. Plans for this drive called for the 79th to make the main effort northwards, with the tested 4th and 9th Divisions covering its flanks. The Division's first D-Day and H-Hour came at 0500, June 19th.

FALL OF CHERBOURG

Good progress was made for two days while the Division accustomed itself to the unforessen [sic] difficulties of hedgerow warfare. The advance was slowed momentarily at the outer defenses of "Fortress Cherbourg", but air bombardment and artillery and naval fire aided in their reduction. At length, however, it was the foot troops who had to carry the ball when Fort du Roule was reached. This fort, a bastion of the Atlantic Wall and termed "impregnable" by Berlin, was the key of the inner defenses of the city. Situated on a rocky height overlooking Cherbourg, honeycombed with corridors and covered with firing ports, it had enough troops and supplies to withstand a long siege. The fury of the 79th's attack, however, was such that the garrison capitulated after only one day of resistance, during which the doughboys blasted their way into tunnels, silenced guns with demolitions, and kept a tremendous stream of fire directed at the ports. On the evening of June 25 came the Fort's formal surrender, followed the next day by that of the city.

KRAUTS CAUGHT NAPPING WHEN 79TH FORGED SEINE BRIDGEHEAD

On June 27 the Division moved south from Cherbourg to relieve elements of the 90th Infantry Division on the extreme right of the Allied line and preparations were begun for a drive south under VIII Corps. The jump-off came on July 3 when the units crossed the Ollonde River and attacked south. The Division's axis of advance led through some of the most difficult terrain it ever traversed — the Norman hedgerow country. German delaying tactics made the greatest possible use of the hedgerows, and, consequently, each pasture frequently developed into a miniature battlefield. North of the Ay River, enemy defenses centered around two important points — La Haye du Puits and Hill 84 — and at both these points the infantry encountered opposition of the toughest nature. Enemy fire was extremely heavy and accurate, enemy tanks were active, and the foot troops had to advance with a minimum of fire support. As La Haye du Puits was cleared house by house, the bulk of its defenders withdrew to a strongpoint in the railroad yards where a last ditch-stand took place before the town was finally cleared on July 9. Simultaneously, at Hill 84 — "Bloody Hill" — the Division met stubborn resistance as it strove to gain possession of this last high ground north of the Ay River. A stiff, see-saw engagement had to be fought through the village of Montgardon before the enemy conceded the Hill to the 79th. On July 13 the enemy withdrew south of the Ay River and the Division halted its advance at the north bank. During the next two weeks it marked time while the plans were made that resulted in the great breakthrough of July 24. In this "Operation Cobra", VIII Corps' role was a limited one at first. It was only after the enemy had been crushed at St. Lo that the Division finally got the green light.

THE BREAKTHROUGH

On July 27 it attacked south in a move to envelop the town of Lessay, a strong enemy position. Little opposition was met, however, although the Division's progress was slowed by extensive minefields. The Division drove on south against little resistance until July 29, when it was ordered to make way for the armored divisions exploiting the break-through. On August 2, as it prepared to follow the 6th Armored Division into Brittany, orders from General Bradley completely changed the Division's mission. It was transferred to the XV Corps in the new Third Army, motorized and ordered to move rapidly on Fougeres. By noon of the following day the town had been captured and preparations were made to defend it against any enemy counterattacks at this critical point in the Allied line.

Note 1: *The paper says the Division was "motorized." It was at this point that the Infantry started on a walking jaunt of approximately 20 miles or more per day, for at least seven days straight, as we tried to keep up with Patton's Armored unit, which was spearheading the drive. ... Motorized my butt!*

Note 2: *This was the first action for General Patton since his combat action in Sicily. As I described before, hen he told General Bradley and the rest of the General Command in Normandy that his intention was to spearhead out and not stop, he was asked what he would do about his open flanks, which would become more and more exposed the further he moved out. He said, "To hell with my flanks, I'll keep kicking the enemy's ass so quick and often they will not know what's happening to them." This was the first time a maneuver like that was tried in modern warfare and ol' General George S. Patton pulled it off. I think it is the village of Laval that has a full size statue of him smack in the center of the village square.*

On August 5 the Division resumed its advance, with the mission of seizing the Mayenne River crossings at Laval. The city was occupied the next day and, following the establishment of bridgeheads on the east bank of the Mayenne, Division engineers quickly installed bridges. The next day the 79th continued its eastward drive, the new objective being the important communications center of Le Mans. Increased opposition was encountered between Laval and Le Mans but on the afternoon of August 8 Division troops entered the main square of the latter city.

The Corps' advance had brought it around to the rear of the enemy facing the British and Americans to the north. On August 9 the Division was ordered to prepare to move northwards behind the 5th Armored Division in a move to make contact with the British, thereby surrounding the German Seventh Army. Following the armor north through Mamers, the 79th reached the vicinity of Le Mele-Sur-Sarthe where it was ordered into Corps reserve. Here on August 14 the Division teamed up with the Air Forces to destroy more than 50 enemy vehicles in which the Germans were attempting to break out of the pocket. On the same day came orders to advance on Versailles.

Note 3: *Versailles is west and just a bit south of the city of Paris. It was possible that the 79th could have been the liberating force to enter the city first, but for political reasons all of the American forces were held back while the French forces under de Gaulle were the ones to move into the city proper.*

ON TO BELGIUM

Motorized again, and moving again with the same speed as the armored divisions on its flanks, the Division reached the Eure River on

August 15. As it made plans to push on to Versailles and beyond to Paris, the 79th's mission was changed again by higher headquarters. Its next objective — the Seine at Mantes-Gassicourt — was designed to block the last important escape route to the east for the enemy caught in Normandy. Enemy resistance to these advances had been spasmodic, and intelligence reports indicated that only light enemy forces were holding the Seine opposite the Division's positions at Mantes-Gassicourt. At 2130 on August 19 came the order to cross and by 0130 elements of the 79th were on the east bank and had secured the first Allied bridgehead beyond the Seine. The bridgehead was expanded to include the river's loop above Mantes-Gassicourt, after which the Division dug in to wait for the inevitable counterattacks.

Note 4: *Earlier in my story, in the section CROSSING THE SEINE, I told how we had been counterattacked after establishing the bridgehead. I covered how the American artillery fired the second highest number of artillery shells in WWII. The artillery guns made the ground rumble and shake to the point that the infantry could hardly sleep. That was two records for one night; the first being the number of shells fired and the second for almost keeping the infantry awake. (The number one record for shells fired in a night, came in March of 1945, at the crossing of the Rhine River.)*

It was also at this crossing of the Seine River that the Germans printed in one of their newspapers that the American forces had dropped paratroopers on the north side of the Seine. Now that crossing was a fast one on our part.

From August 22 to August 26 the enemy strove in vain to close this hole in his defenses around Paris. The 18th GAF Division, with powerful tank support, was decimated by anti-tank fire and the massed fire of Division and Corps Artillery.

On August 30 came the break-out, and, under First Army and XIX Corps, the motorized 79th headed for the Belgian frontier. In seventy-two hours the Division flashed 180 miles across World War I's battlefields to chalk up a new record. In the words of the Corps Commander, it was "one of the fastest opposed advances by an Infantry Division in the history of warfare." From September 2 to 5 the Division waited for new orders at its assembly area near Sameon on the Franco-Belgian frontier and a day later it started south to rejoin Third Army and XV Corps.

Note 5: *In actuality, we stopped at the French-Belgian border because high command decided to switch all supplies to the new operation as they were seeking to spearhead into Germany. Years later this operation was covered by the movie "A Bridge Too Far." The "Bridge Too Far" was British General Montgomery's brainchild and it failed, costing the Allied forces approximately 10,000 troops. (You cannot move tanks and infantry division without gasoline.) The title of the movie takes its name from the British officer's comment. While listening to the strategic command laying out the whole operation of taking five bridges in Holland, he made the remark, "Maybe you are going a bridge too far?" (meaning "Are you biting off more than you can chew?") His words were prophetic.*

ANOTHER BREAKTHROUGH

By September 9 the Division had assembled in its new locations near Joinville, with bridgeheads established over the Marne River. Here it was in position to block any move against Third Army's south flank by the enemy retreating up the Rhone Valley before the Seventh U.S. Army. However, on September 11 the Division's eastward advance was resumed. Moving across the entire front of the German 16th Infantry Division, one of the combat teams drove sixty miles to cross the Meuse and reach the outskirts of Charmes.

Note 6: *I covered my role in the taking of the city of Charmes in the body of this document, under the title "Now For The Top Of The Hill."*

The other combat teams peeled off the Division's column to wipe out enemy garrisons parallel to this route, at Poussay and Mirecourt and at Neufchateau. After short but stubborn battles these towns were captured and on September 15 the whole Division assembled at Charmes to support the bridgehead secured on the east bank of the Moselle. On September 18 the advance was resumed and next day the Division crossed the Mortagne against slight opposition. Two days later, however, heavy resistance was met when patrols came up against strong enemy positions along the Meurthe. After eight weeks of flight, the Germans had succeeded in stopping their rout and, until the next breakthrough, two months later, they gave ground only after bitter resistance.

From September 19 to 23 the enemy strongly contested all attempts of the Division to break the Meurthe River line. On the left flank, one combat team cleared the enemy from Luneville, thereby jeopardizing the Nazi right flank, and the next day the Germans withdrew to new defensive positions along the Vezouse River and through the Foret de Parroy. Reconnaissance indicated that the enemy was holding the forest in strength and Sound and Flash units reported a considerable concentration of enemy artillery to the east. The Division planned to attack following a heavy bombardment of the forest by XIX T.A.C. but poor weather forced this to be postponed until September 28. When it did come off, it was hardly a success, and the first foot troops into the forest encountered tough resistance. The thickness of the forest, the well dug-in and experienced enemy troops of the 15th Panzer Grenadier Division, and their heavy supporting fire, all combined to make the Division's progress slow and costly. But the forest had do [sic] be taken and it was. On October 9 a carefully planned attack was launched and after heavy fighting the enemy was driven from his commanding positions in the middle of the forest. Next day the enemy evacuated to new positions on high ground to the east of the forest with the Division closely following up the withdrawal. Two weeks later the 79th was relieved by the 44th Infantry Division for its first break in 128 days of combat. The Division assembled in rest areas around Luneville and made plans for the next campaign.

Note 7: *The first night after leaving the wonderful security of the rest area we found ourselves just inside of the enemy artillery range. We knew that because we had walked past our own dug in artillery. Just prior to us getting there, our artillery had received some counter-fire from the Krauts and there were a few American bodies lying on the ground. Some of the new replacements that we had with us started looking around nervously and saying, "Look at that ... look at that." I recall that I yelled at them to "Look ahead and shut your damn mouths, just keep moving!"*

I don't know if it was the next morning or the one after that, but we woke up in the morning with about half an inch of snow over all of the landscape, including us. We didn't have a cover over our holes as we had dug only slit trenches to sleep in. We were well camouflaged until we stood up and then we stood out like black thumbs on a white landscape. Winter was upon us.

CLEARING OF ALSACE

Seventh Army and XV Corps plans called for a breaking of the German lines in Lorraine, the forcing of a passage through the Vosges and the clearing of the enemy from Alsace. The enemy was established in strong positions along the Vezouse and was preparing an even stronger defense line along the heights of the Vosges where he hoped to hold through the winter. To the 79th was assigned the task of forcing a breakthrough which would be exploited by the 2nd French Armored Division. On November 13 the Division returned to the line, and attacked northeast from the vicinity of Harbouey. In a week of heavy fighting it drove a deep wedge into the enemy's lines, and, "fighting like devils", in the words of a French report, succeeded in forcing a passage of the Vezouse. The French armor poured through the hole in the enemy's lines and uncovered the brilliant maneuver that pierced the Vosges and freed Strasbourg. The 79th followed up, clearing Phalsbourg, and moving into Alsace to cover the French at Strasbourg from the north.

The Division then dug in near Brumath and awaited the opening of the next offensive. This began on December 9 when the 79th, now under VI Corps, attacked to the northeast along the Rhine with the objective of breaching the Siegfried Line. Haguenau and Bischwiller were seized and after overcoming stubborn enemy delaying action the 79th reached the frontier along the Lauter River on December 15. The attack was pressed and the Division drove on into Germany to reach the formidable defenses of the enemy's West Wall. Advance reports of its strength proved accurate, for the Division met a hail of fierce fire. But after brisk fighting a foothold was gained inside the Line itself. Suddenly came the order to withdraw to the Lauter River as Higher Headquarters reshuffled the Western Front to meet the enemy's Ardennes threat. On December 22 and 23 this was accomplished and Christmas was observed by the troops as they outposted defensive positions along the river. Then the enemy unveiled another threat in the West – this time just to the west of the 79th's positions – and on January 2nd another withdrawal had to be made by the Division to new positions based on the Maginot Line. Four battalions were loaned temporarily to the adjacent 45th Division on the right, as it strove to contain the enemy's thrust, and, in return, Corps attached to the 79th Task Force Linden (the three regiments of the 42nd Infantry Division). The Division prepared for the inevitable enemy follow-up, improving its Maginot positions and keeping a close watch on the right flank along the Rhine. On January 6 came the first of the enemy's attacks.

DEFENSE OF ALSACE

The importance the enemy attached to this offensive was graphically disclosed as identifications of his units rolled in: 21st Panzer Division, 25th Panzer Grenadier Division and 7th Parachute Division. The first of these crack veteran units effected a penetration of the Maginot positions near Hatten on January 9 and through this slot the enemy poured men and armor to surround this village and the next one to the west, Rittershoffen. A battalion of the 79th clung on in each of these villages in the face of overwhelming German strength and fire. The enemy hurled attack after attack at these two battalions, and his two other divisions appeared to relieve the 21st Panzer. Meanwhile, on the Division's right flank along the Rhine, the enemy had secured a bridgehead and had been able to build it up with considerable strength, including his excellent 10th SS Panzer Division. Untested American units were forced to withdraw in the face of their assault, and, as the situation deteriorated, it became apparent that a withdrawal would have to be made to a new MLR along the Moder River. Accordingly, Hatten and Rittershoffen were evacuated successfully on the night of January 20 and the Division established its new positions on the Moder. The enemy was slow to follow up this move, and it was not until the night of January 24 that he attempted to assault the new line. The parachute, panzer grenadier and SS panzer divisions all secured bridgeheads on the south bank of the river, but at an extremely costly price. The numbers of enemy dead and wounded ran high and the Division's PW Cage was filled many times over. The next day the Germans called it quits and pulled back to the north of the river. On February 7 the Division was relieved in its positions by the 36th and 101st Divisions and assembled at Pont-a-Mousson for a rest.

On February 14 the Division was alerted for a rail and motor move northwards to join Ninth Army and XVI Corps and five days later the units closed into new areas in the vicinity of Tongres, Belgium. Much later it was revealed that this move had been made so that the 79th would be set and on the spot when the time came for an assault crossing of the Rhine. In the meanwhile, the Division played a limited role as the final operations to clear the Rhineland took place. In the American offensive which began on February 23, only one of the combat teams participated, clearing a sector east of Heinsberg to the Roer River. After the breakthrough had been effected, the Division passed to XIII Corps and on March 1 was given the mission of safeguarding the Corps rear areas as it sped across the Rhine plain. On March 7, however, came the order to return to Holland (and XVI Corps) to make ready for the great task ahead – "Operation Flashpoint", the crossing of the Rhine. Sites along the Maas were selected as best matching conditions at the Rhine, and for two weeks the Division carried out a training program in river-crossing operations. Meticulous plannning [sic] took into consideration all possible developments and angles, and plans were made to fire the greatest artillery preparation of the war. In perfect weather the Air Forces saturated the east bank of the Rhine and on the evening of March 23 the last moves forward were made.

THE RHINE CROSSING

At 0300, March 24, following the hour-long artillery preparation laid down by sixteen battalions of field artillery the Division's two assault battalions jumped off. Against little resistance, the east bank was reached and bridgeheads secured. At once the build-up commenced, with men and equipment being ferried across the river by all manner of army and navy craft. By evening the city of Dinslaken had been captured after a stiff fight and the 79th had gained a large foothold on the east bank. Following the build-up, the Division swung south and drove for the Rhine-Herne Canal. Spasmodic resistance was met and on March 30 the Canal was reached after the 79th had overrun countless towns, including the imoprtant [sic] city of Duisburg-Hamborn.

The Ninth Army objective, however, had not yet been seized and the 79th was again earmarked for a spearhead role. Ninth Army was to close up to the Ruhr River, there to await the arrival of First Army units pushing up from the south. The 79th would break across the canal and drive into the Ruhr valley. On April 7 it attacked across the Canal near Gelsenkirchen in the face of scattered German opposition. Two days later it was on its objective, the north bank of the Ruhr River, after which followed the clearing of the industrial cities of Bochum, Muhlheim and parts of Essen. On April 16 First Army units uncovered the Division in its positions along the Rhur [sic] and the 79th lost contact with the enemy in the ETO. Thereafter followed military government assignments, first in the Bochum area, and later in an area expanded to the east to include Arnsberg and Lippstadt. Late in May, elements of the British Second Army arrived to establish their permanent military occupation and the 79th was ordered to relieve Third Army units occupying Cheb, Czechoslovakia and part of the surrounding Sudetenland.

❖

I believe this article will give the reader a feeling of the division's accomplishments along with an insight that my division was utilized as a spearhead division to attack on land, to cross rivers, to take and hold the high grounds. Because of this, we moved by sometimes-forced marches, walking and being trucked and being assigned and reassigned to the different Armies and Corps units. We didn't know any of this at the time we were doing it. All we knew was that we were tired (and I mean drag-ass tired) and hungry (enough to eat grain from growing wheat in a field), that we saw more dead and wounded than a noncombatant would believe, and that we were scared shitless more times than we could count. Peace, love and God Bless!